Winnie McGoo's
Museum Adventure

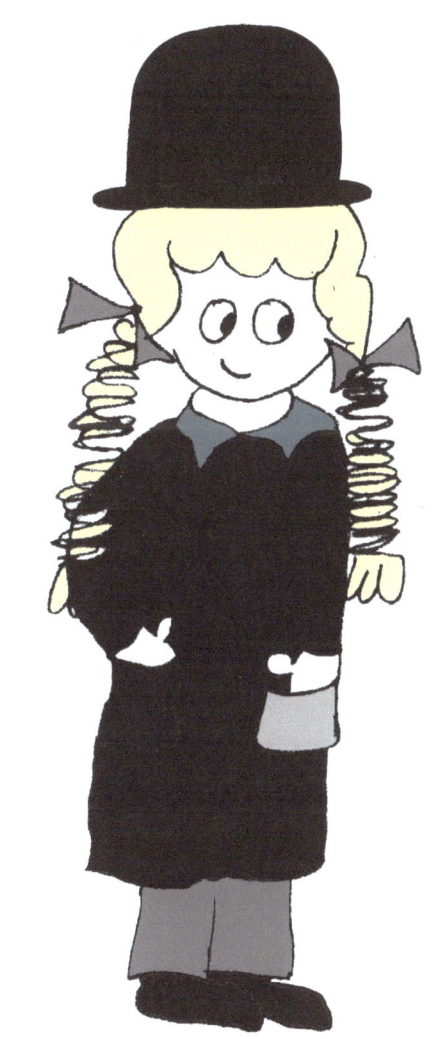

Written and Illustrated by Leslie Nazarian

LesrubaBooks.com

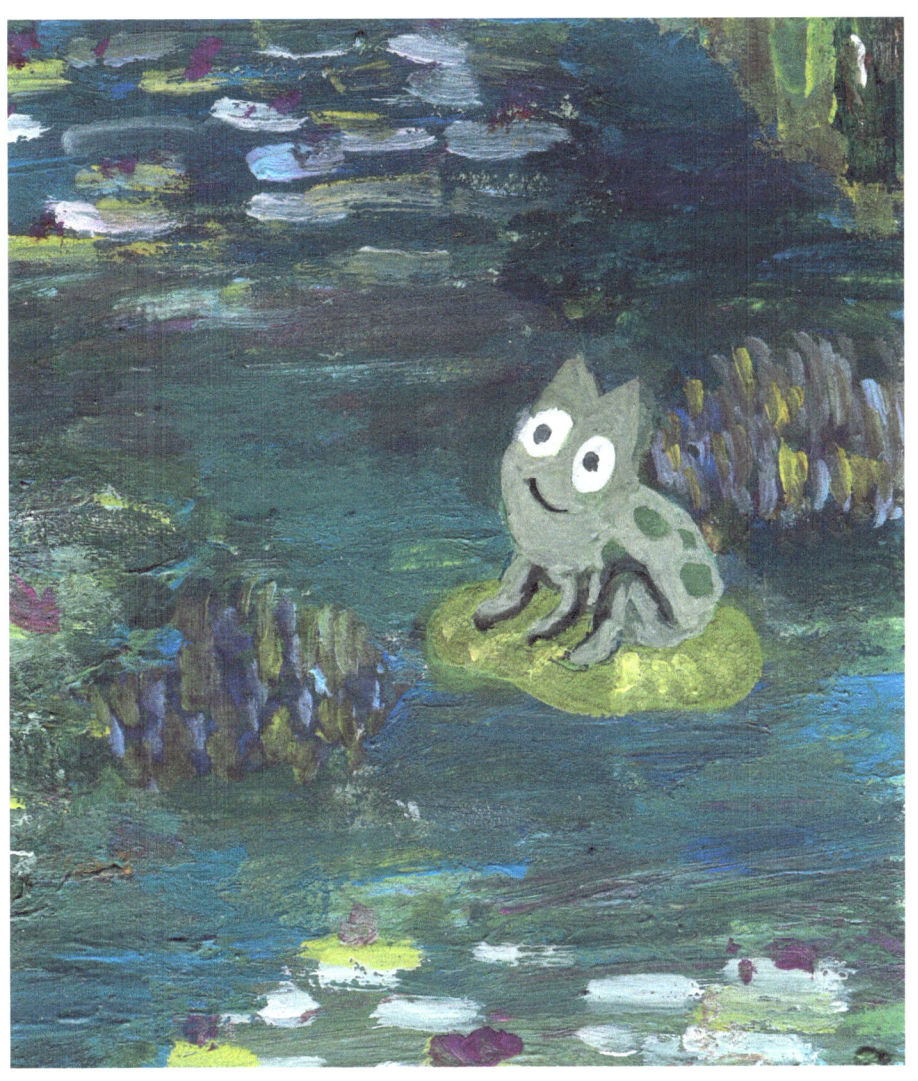

Did you ever sit on a lily pad

Dreaming of things you wish you had?

Like a rocket, a ship, perhaps even some wings,

Or a crown worn by emperors, princes and kings?

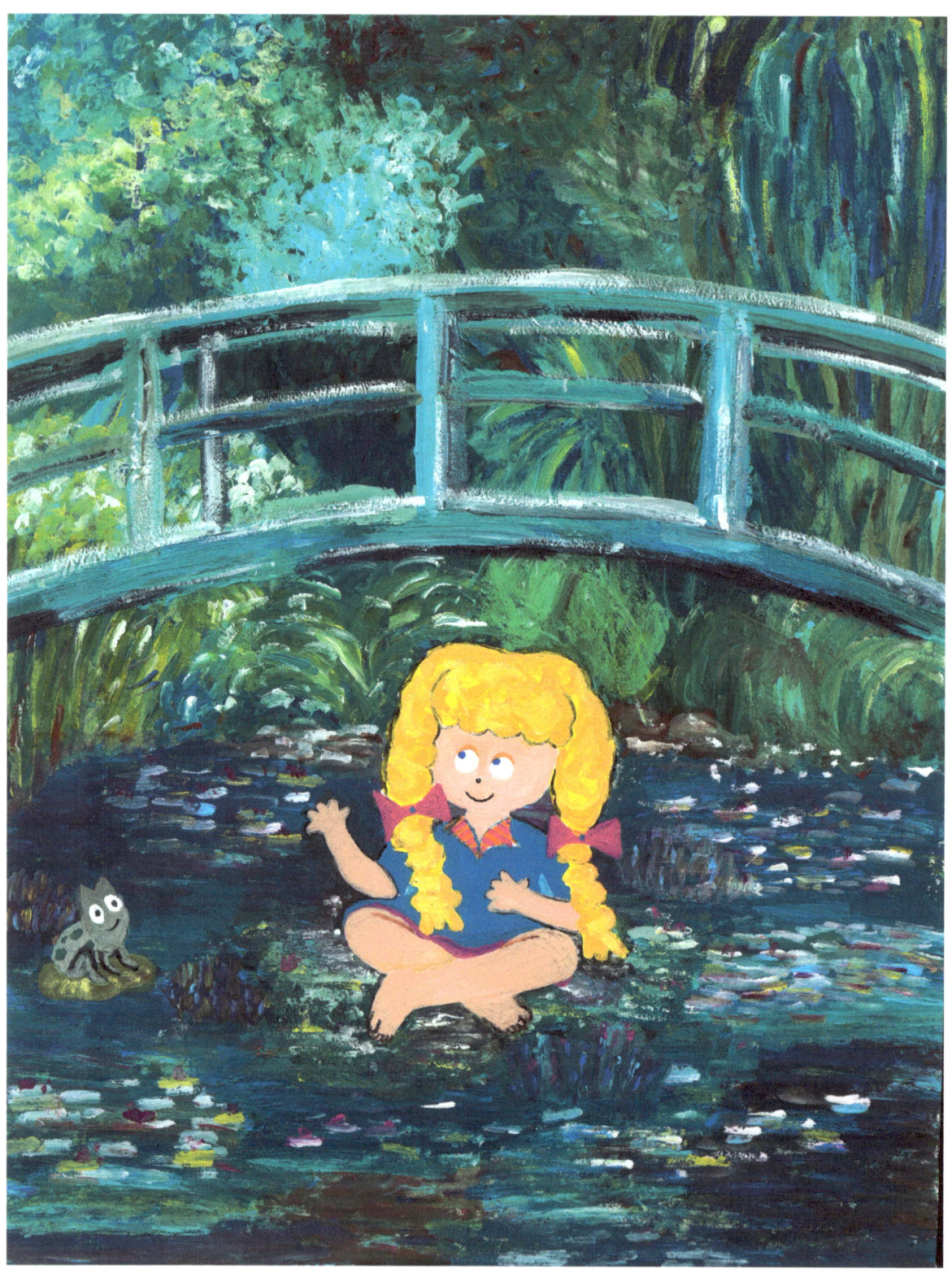

Winnie McGoo had a day just like that.

Where she climbed on a lily pad and for hours just sat.

Dreaming of places far and away,

Winnie McGoo could have sat there all day.

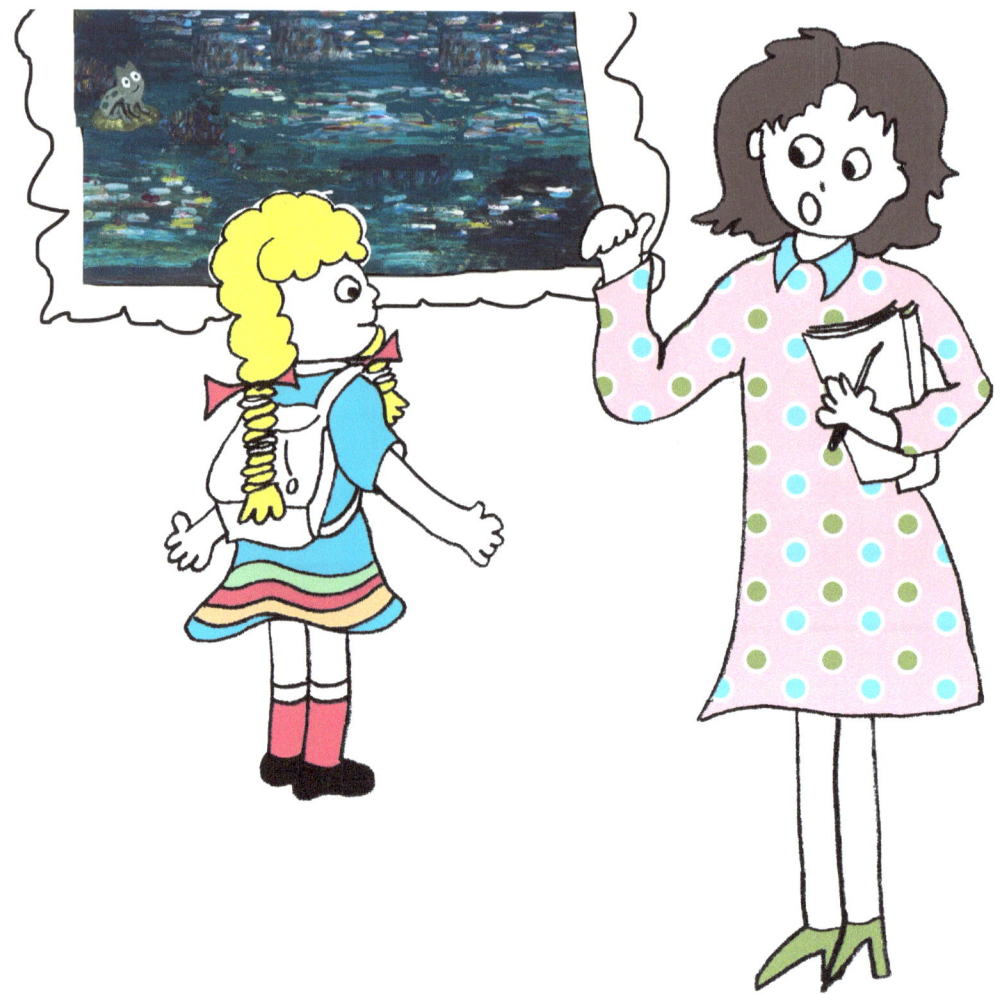

"Winnie, let's go," she heard someone yell.

Pulling her out of her pondering spell.

"Not yet," Winnie said. "I'd much rather stay

and look more at this painting by Claude Monet."

"The museum's going to close," her teacher said, "We must leave."

But Winnie McGoo had a trick up her sleeve.

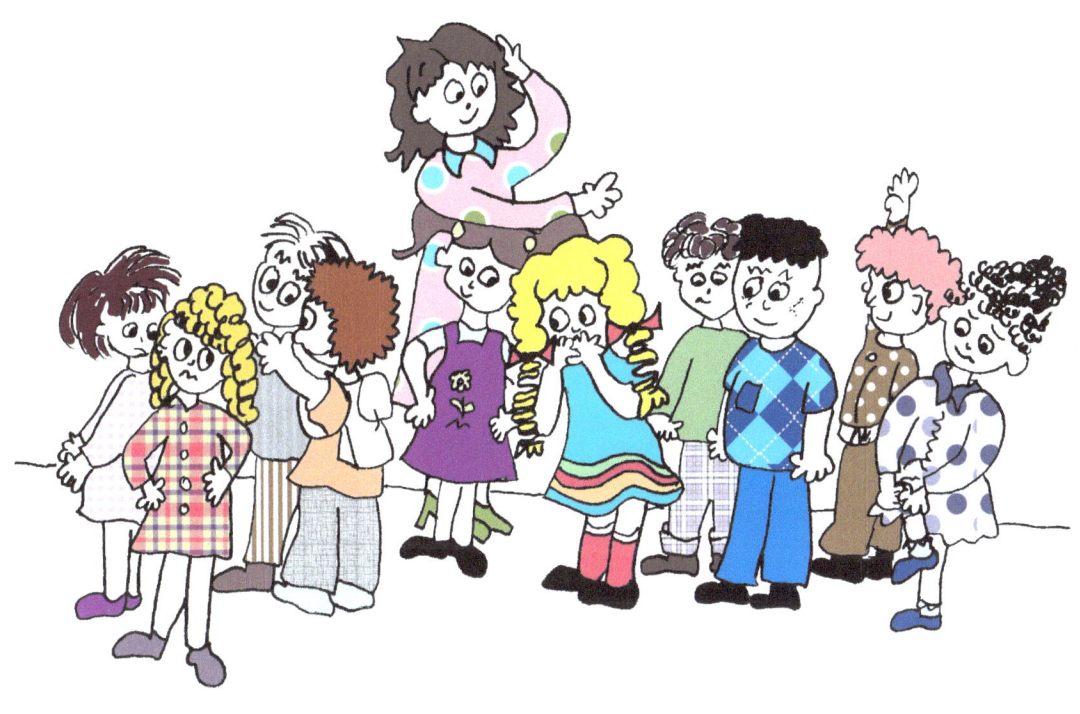

So as her teacher, Miss Bleacher, began counting off,

Winnie McGoo started loudly to cough.

Causing Miss Bleacher to miscount by one,

Winnie sneaked quietly off for more fun.

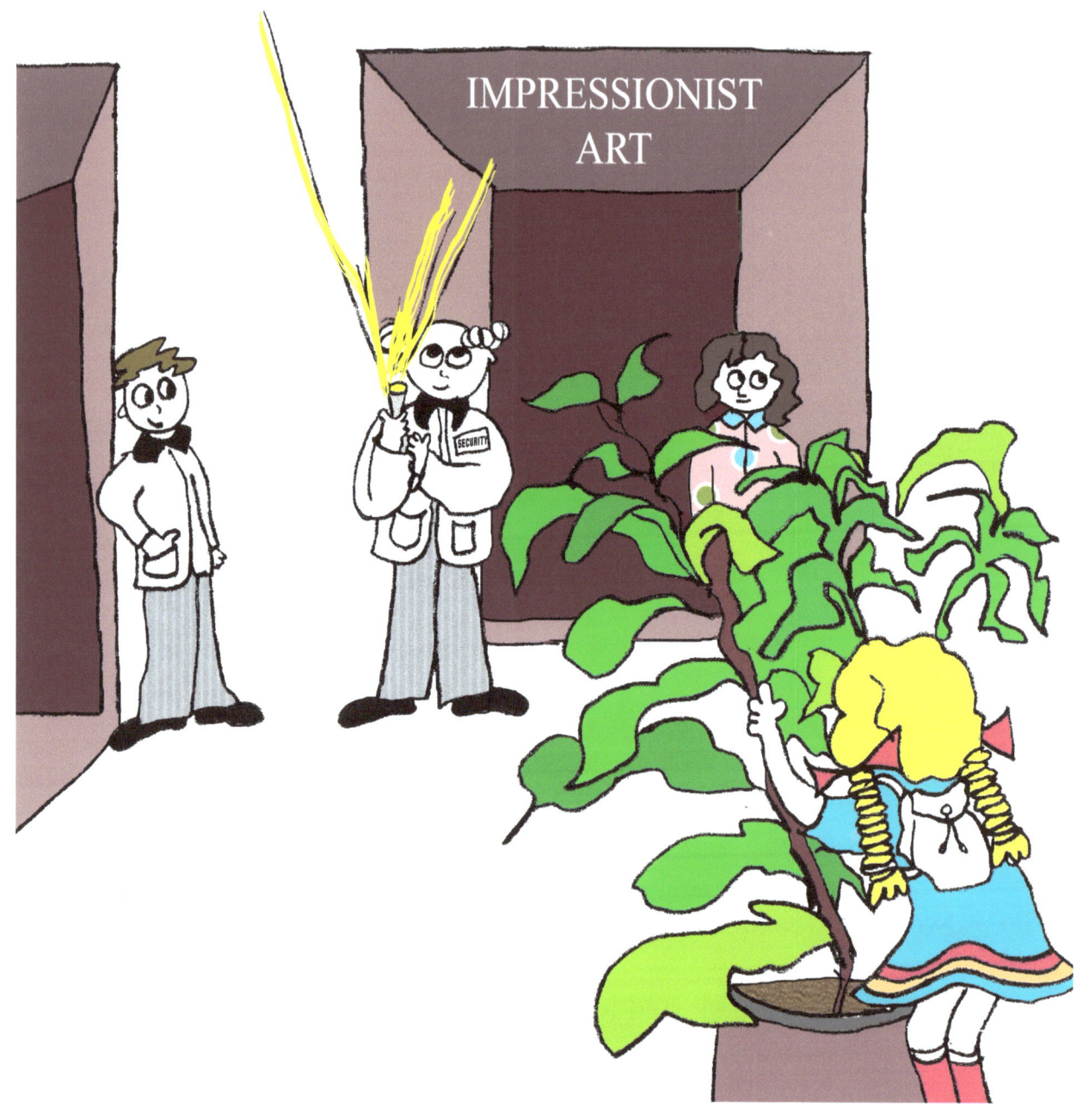

The silence grew heavy, as the visitors left.

Guards took their posts to prevent any theft.

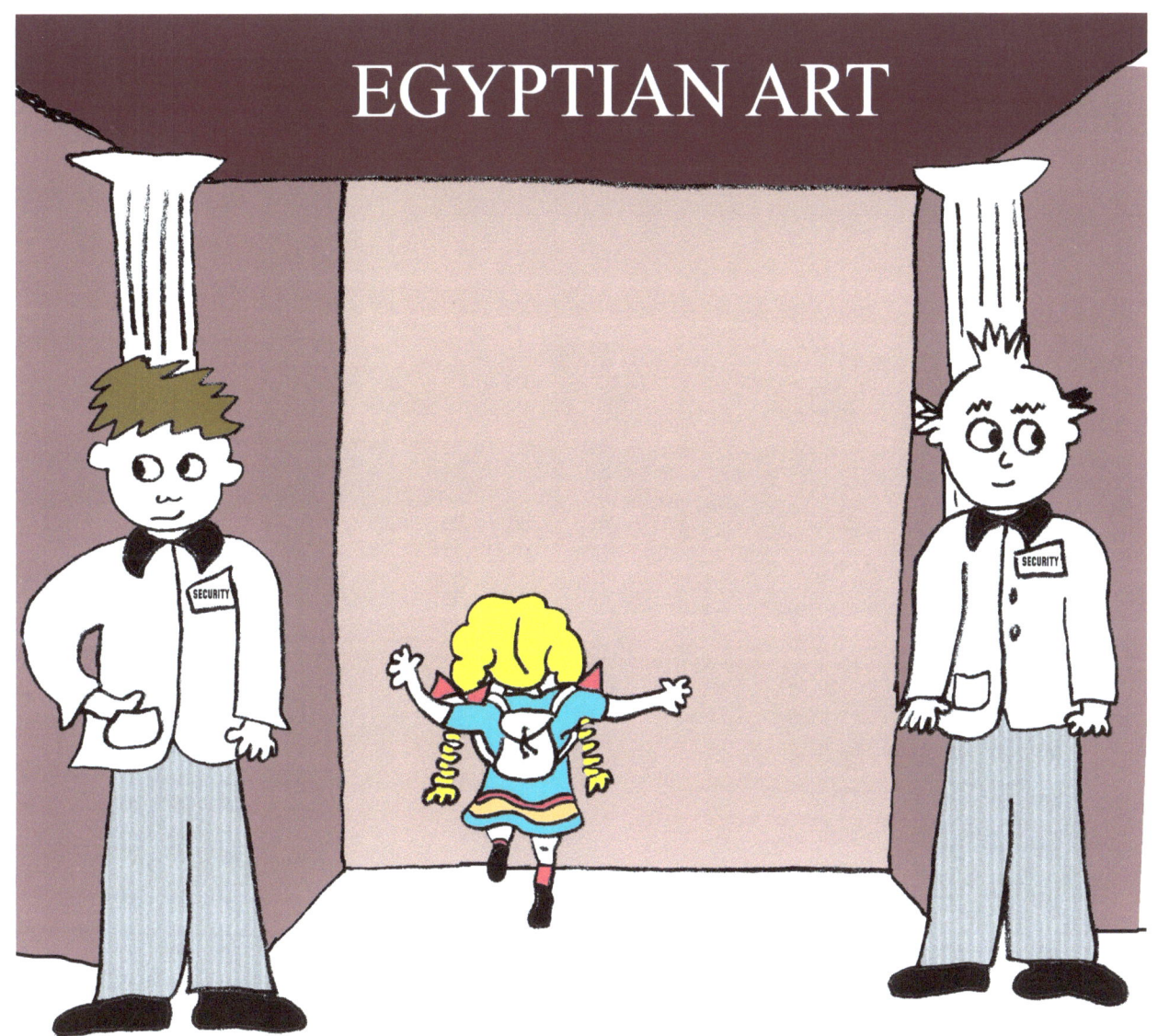

Quiet as could be, Winnie gingerly stepped

To the wing where the pharaohs and mummies were kept.

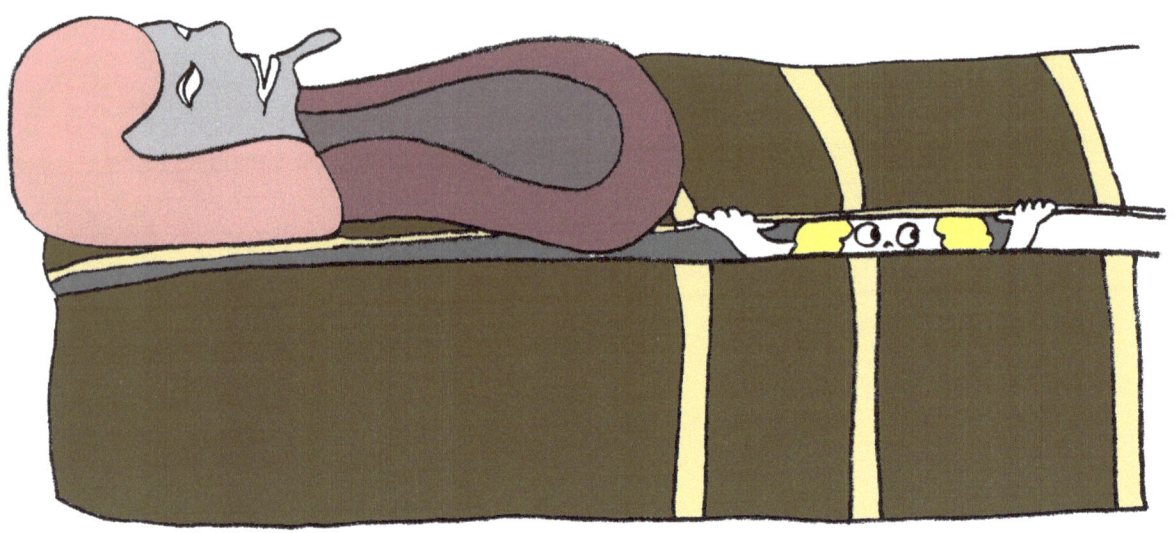

Spooked by a sphinx, Winnie tripped on a nut

and had to hide from a guard in the tomb of King Tut.

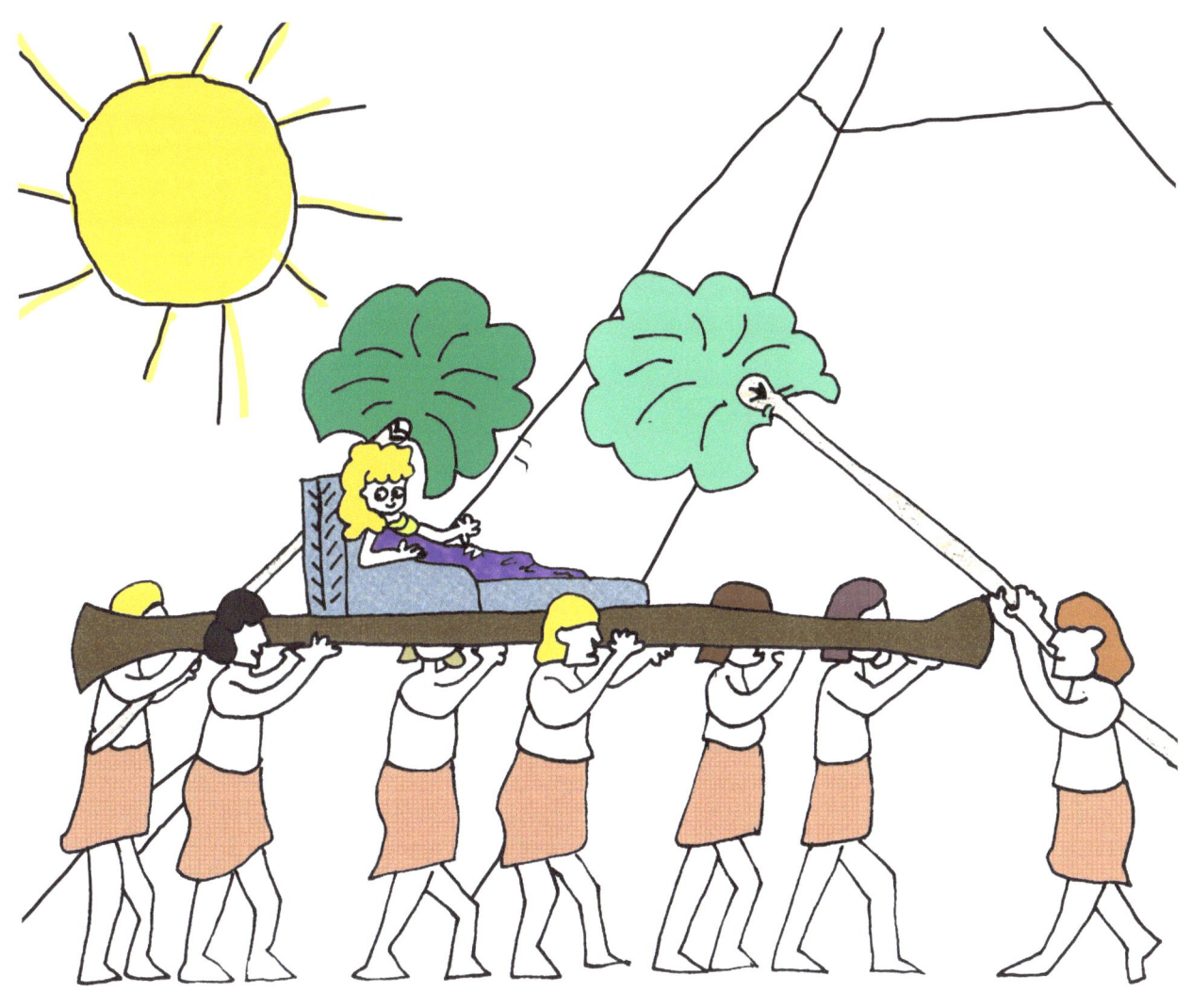

Carting her to Egypt where she got a look first hand

at the great ancient pyramids and WOW were they grand.

The Egyptians mistook her for the Queen of the Nile.

Winnie didn't disappoint them, she just agreed with a smile.

From the hot, dry desert, she headed to Grande Jatte,

an Isle Seurat painted using only the dot.

Winnie smelled the sweet grass and felt the sun shining bright,

but these people, she thought, were not dressed at all right.

Swimsuits and shorts would be far more relaxing.

These tight petticoat corsets they wore were too taxing.

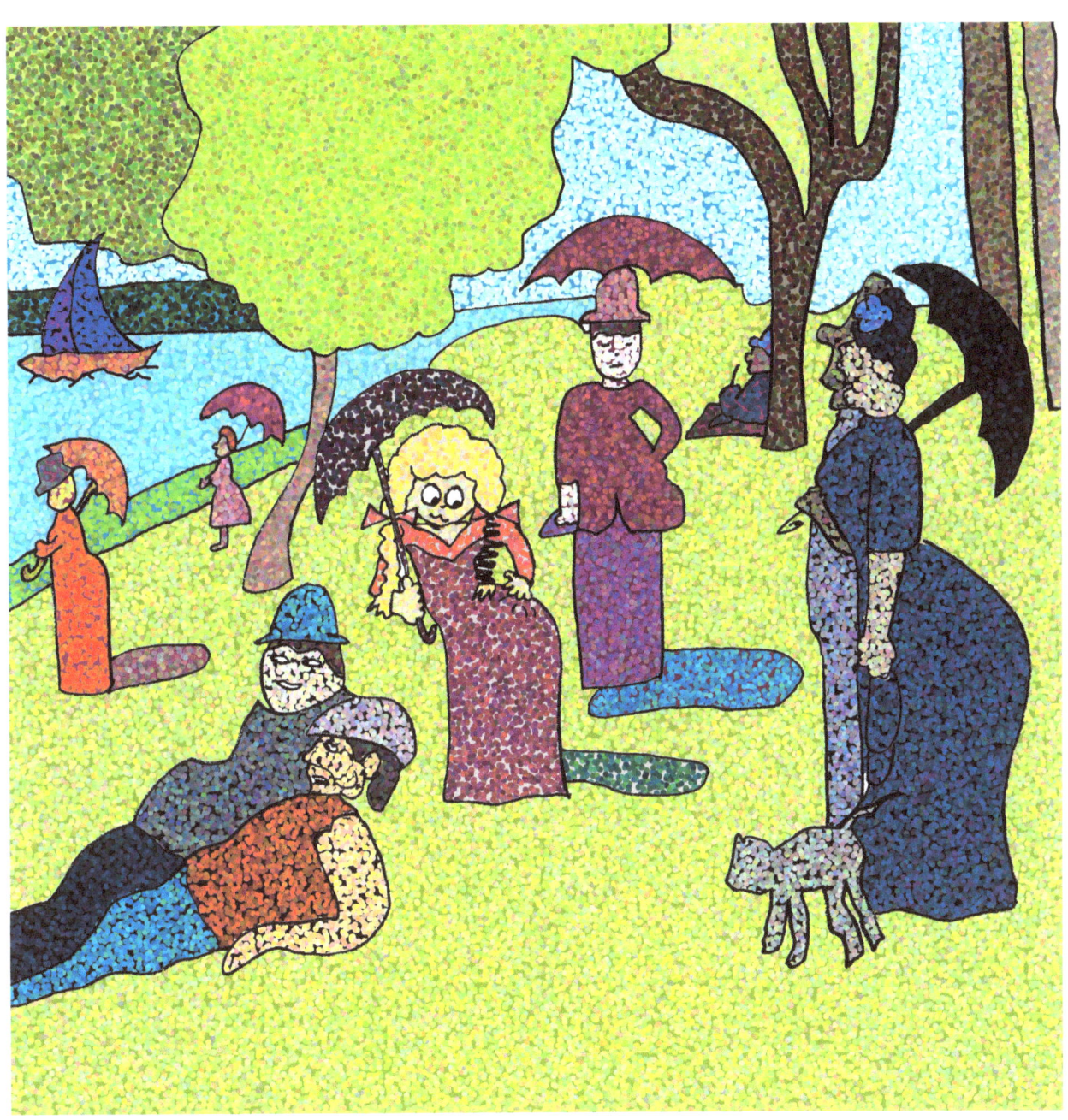

Winnie heard heavy footsteps and went for a dip

to hide from the guard, though he did feel a drip.

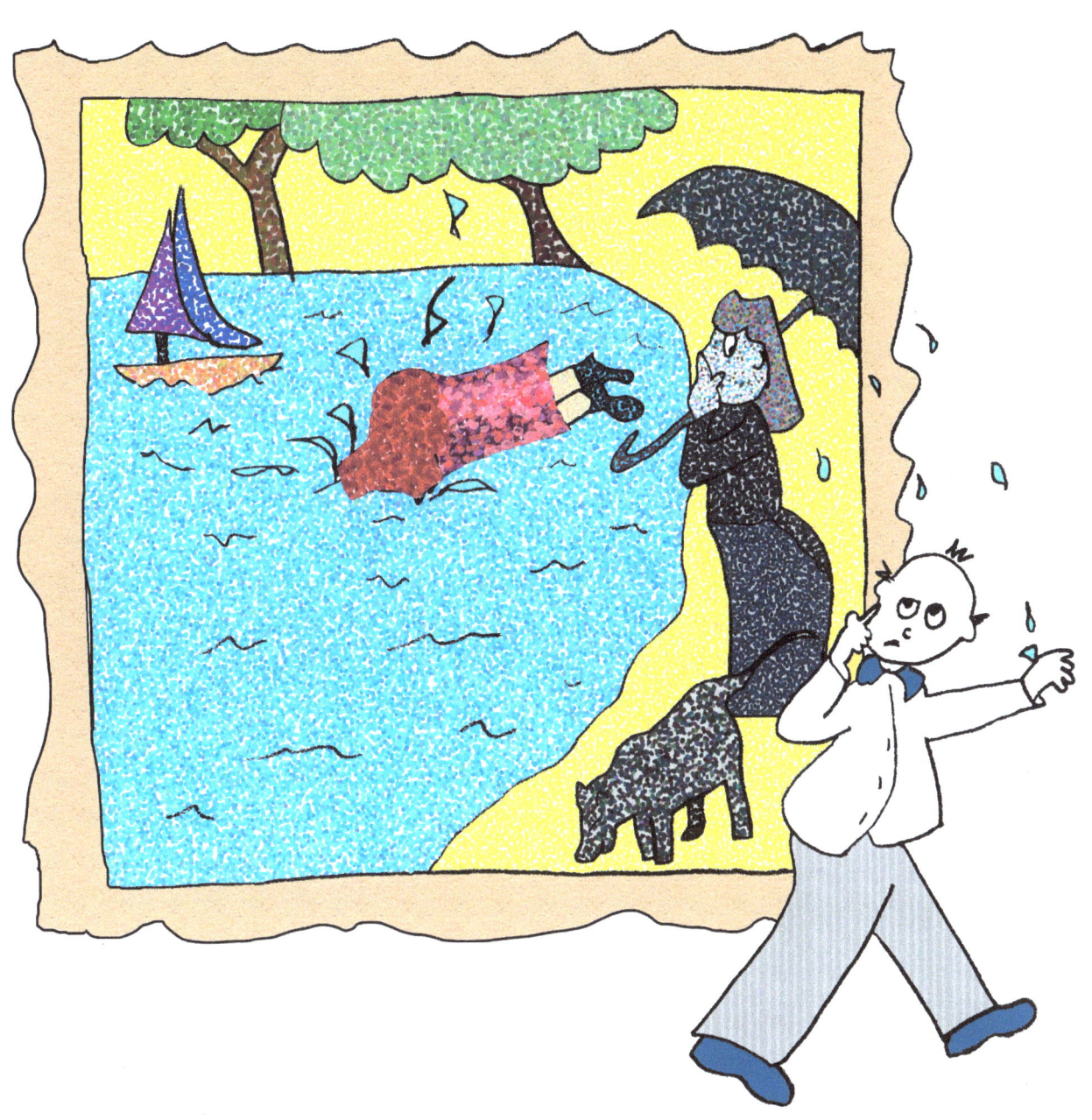

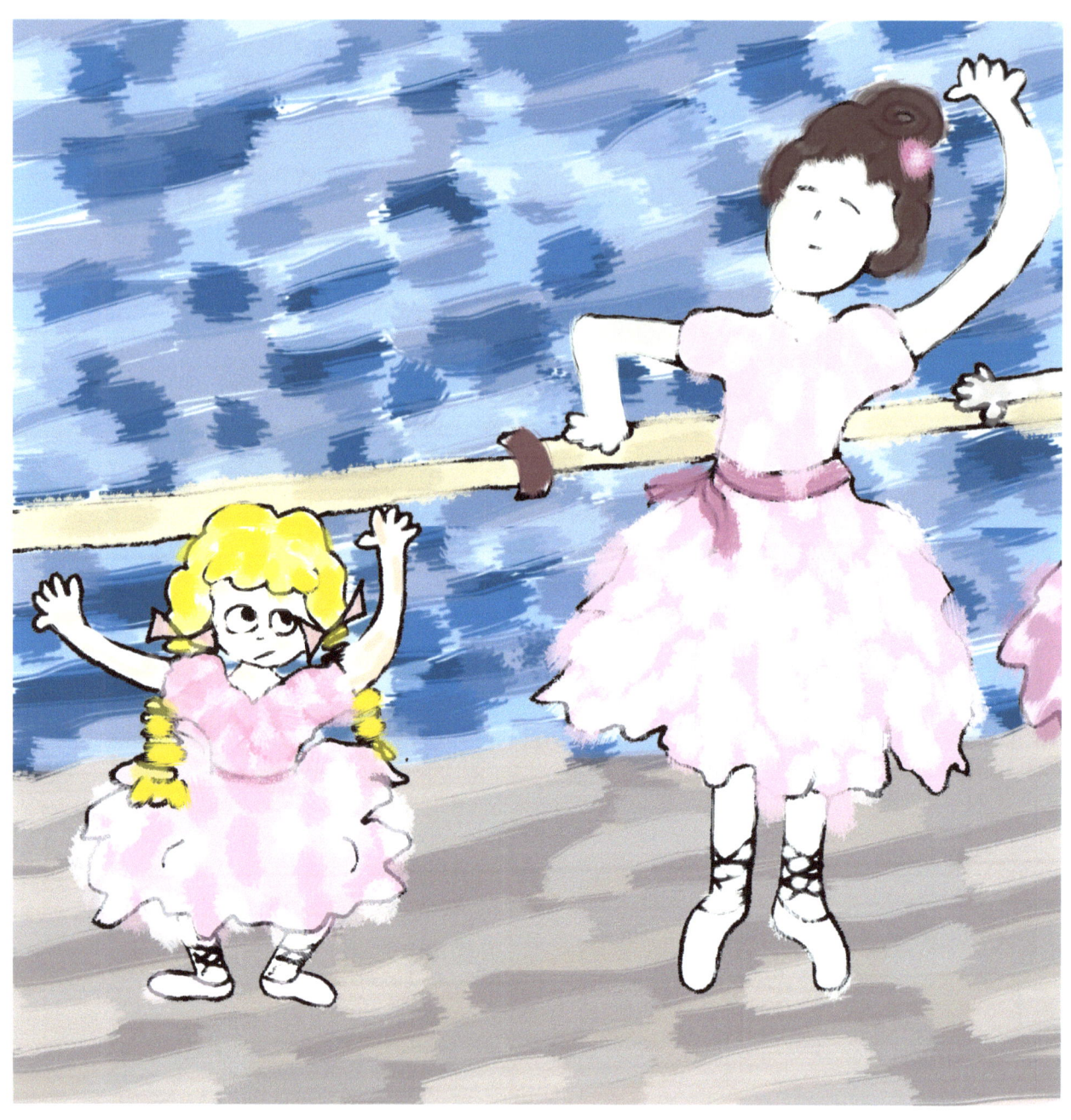

Changing into a tutu, Winnie performed a plié

with Degas' ballerinas in a class of ballet.

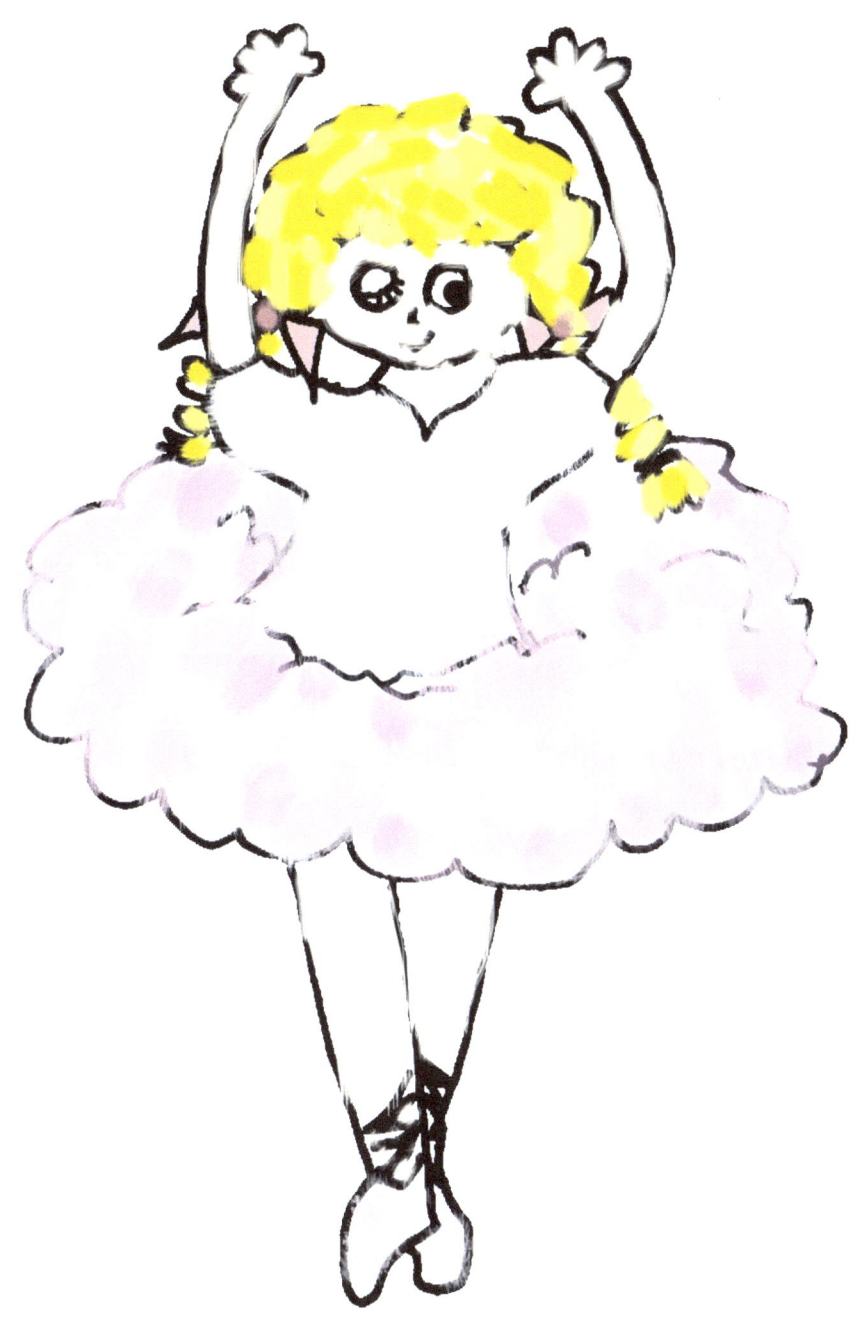

Twirling and swirling so graceful and spry,

Winnie winked at the guard when his gaze caught her eye.

Dancing made her thirsty, so she sipped a frappé

Under twinkling stars at a Renoir café.

Folks were dancing, romancing, passing time with a friend,

music played softly, Winnie didn't want it to end.

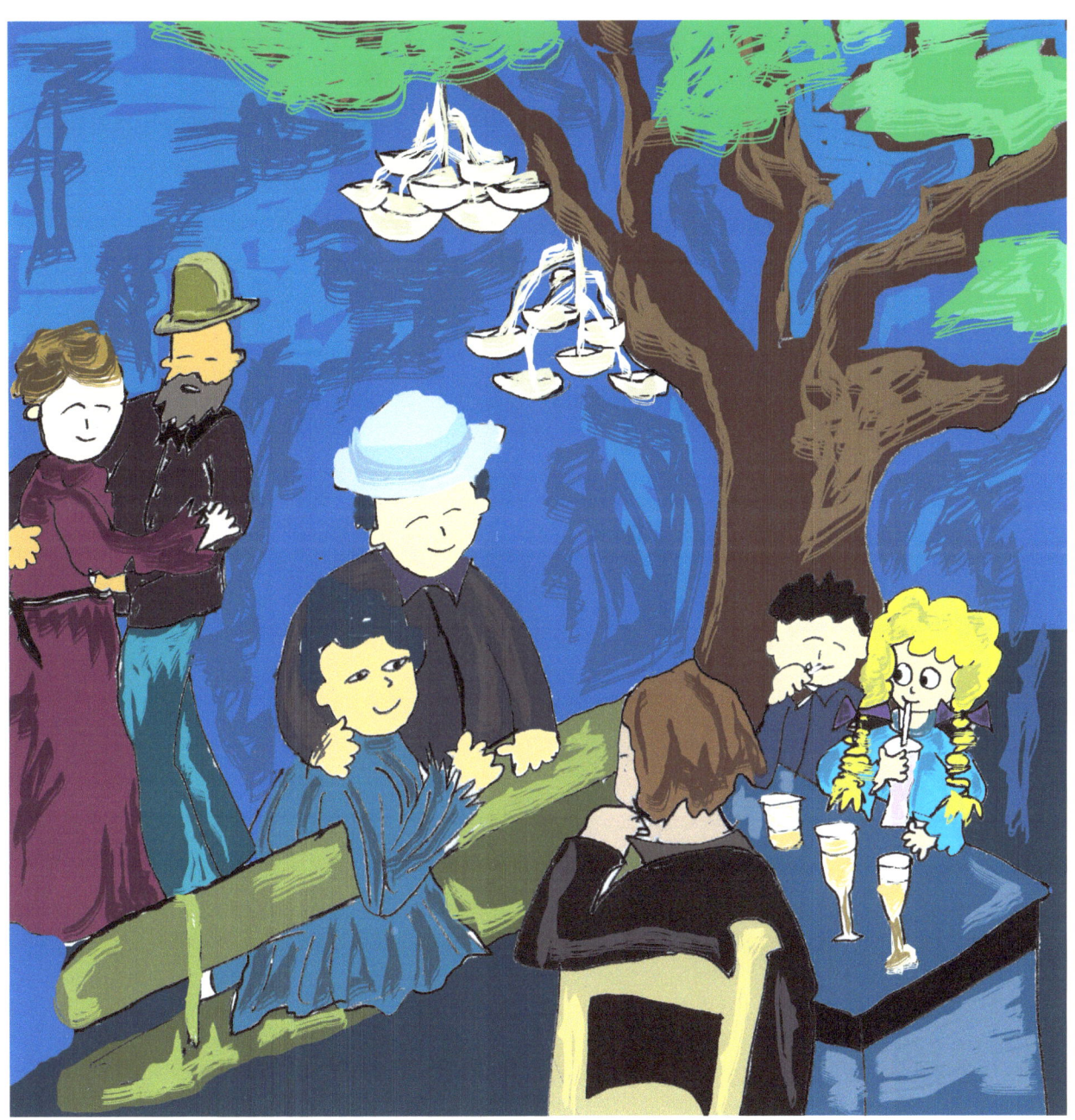

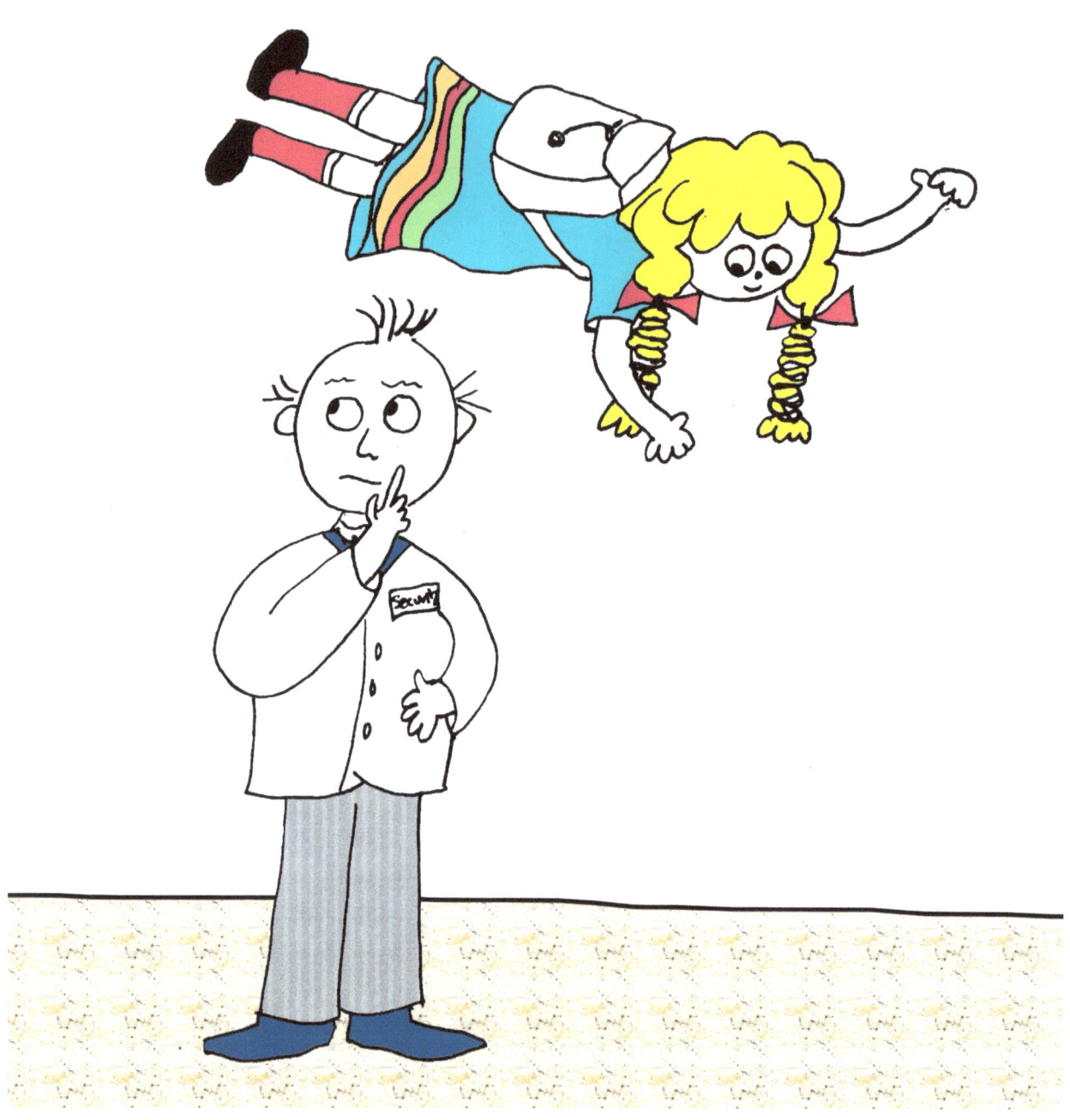

Then the painter, Chagall, lifted her high off the ground,

so when the guard came by she did not make a sound.

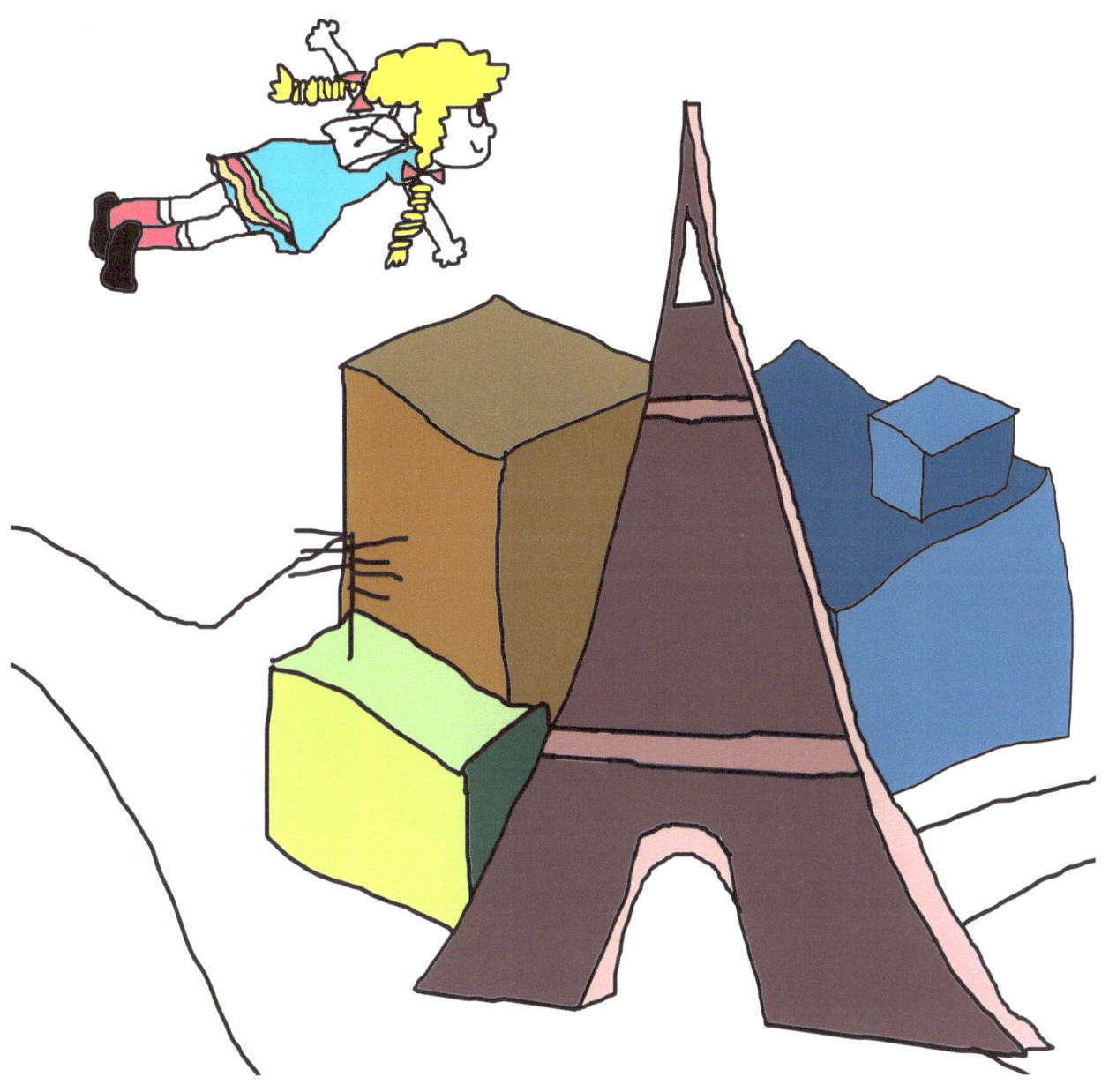

Over rooftops and bridges, Winnie soared through the air.

Floating free as a bird, flying free without care.

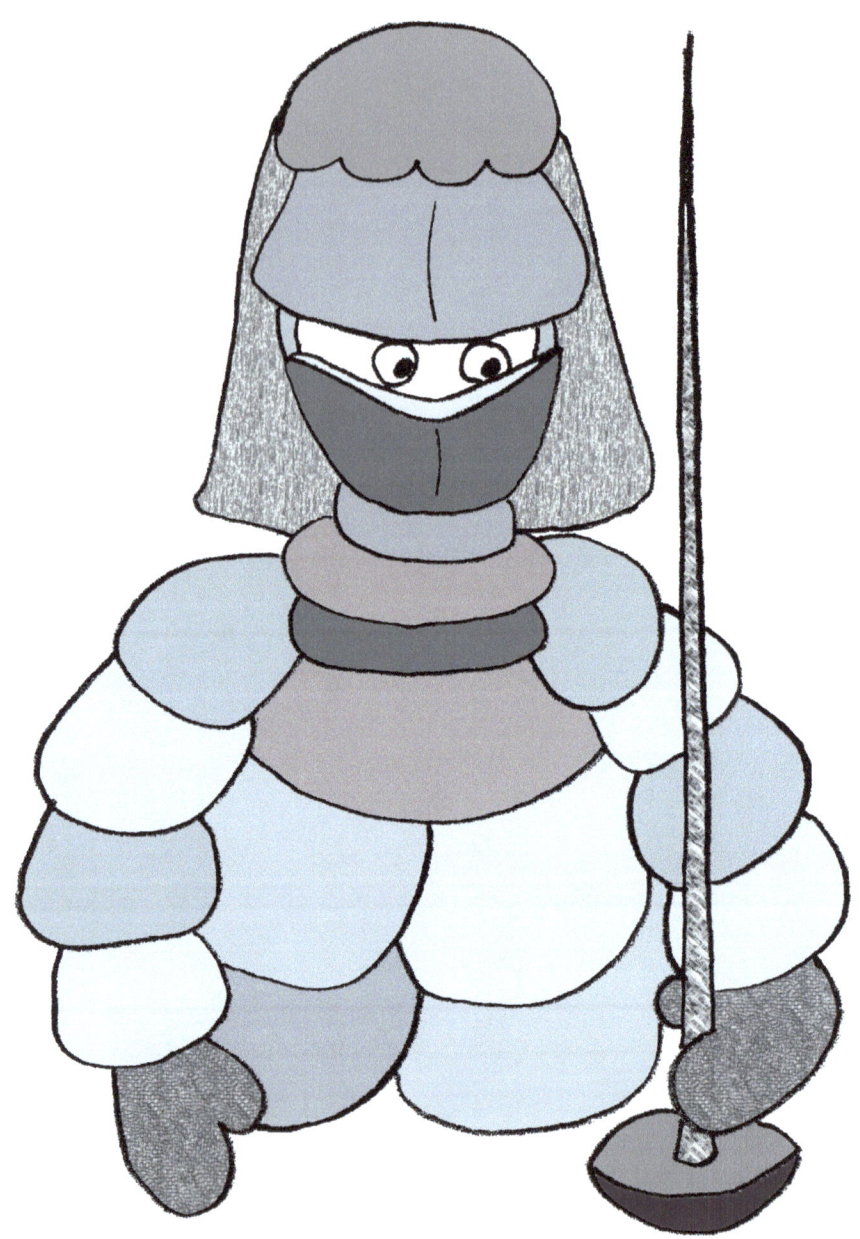

Coming in for a landing in the Medieval wing,

Winnie stopped in her tracks at the sound of a ring.

Staying perfectly hidden in the shell of a knight,

it took her to places that caused quite a fright.

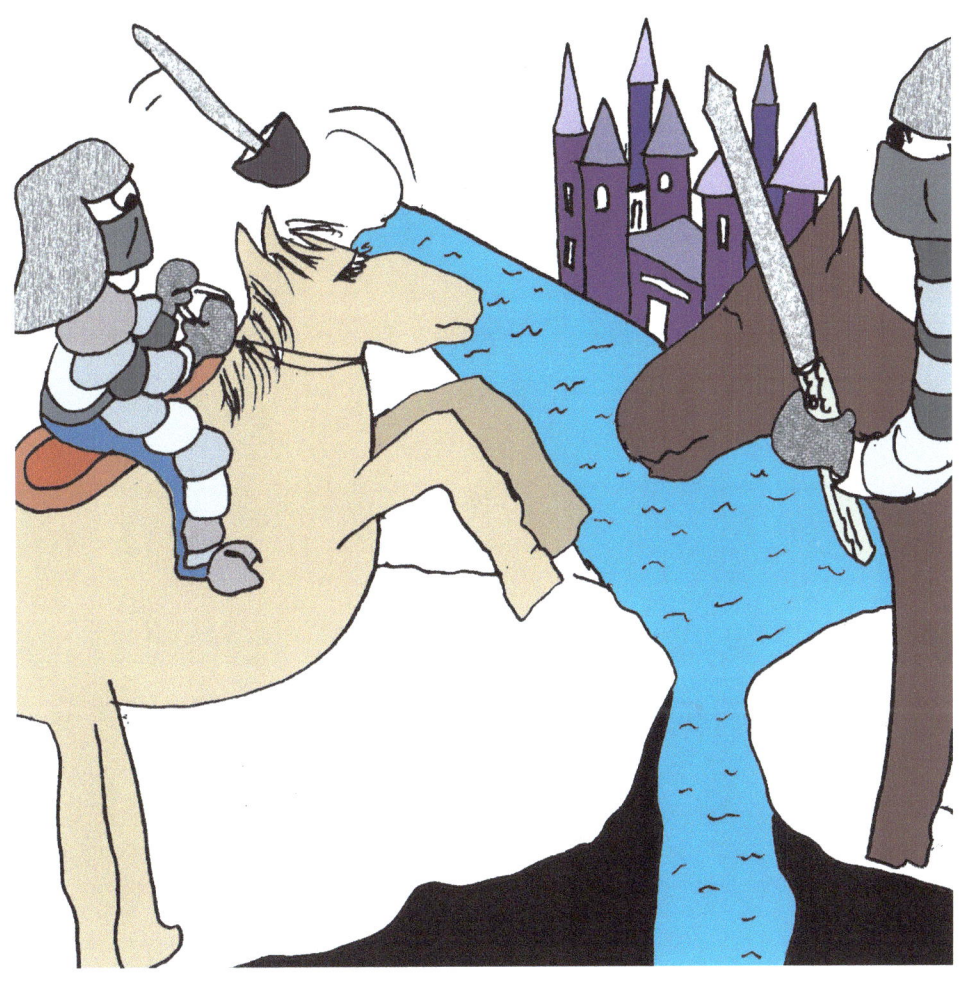

She arrived just in time to storm an old castle,

but weighted in armor was a bit of a hassle.

Riding a horse just made matters worse,

so when the jousting began she fled into reverse.

Escaping the scene and an opponent most mean,

Winnie considered this costume for next Halloween.

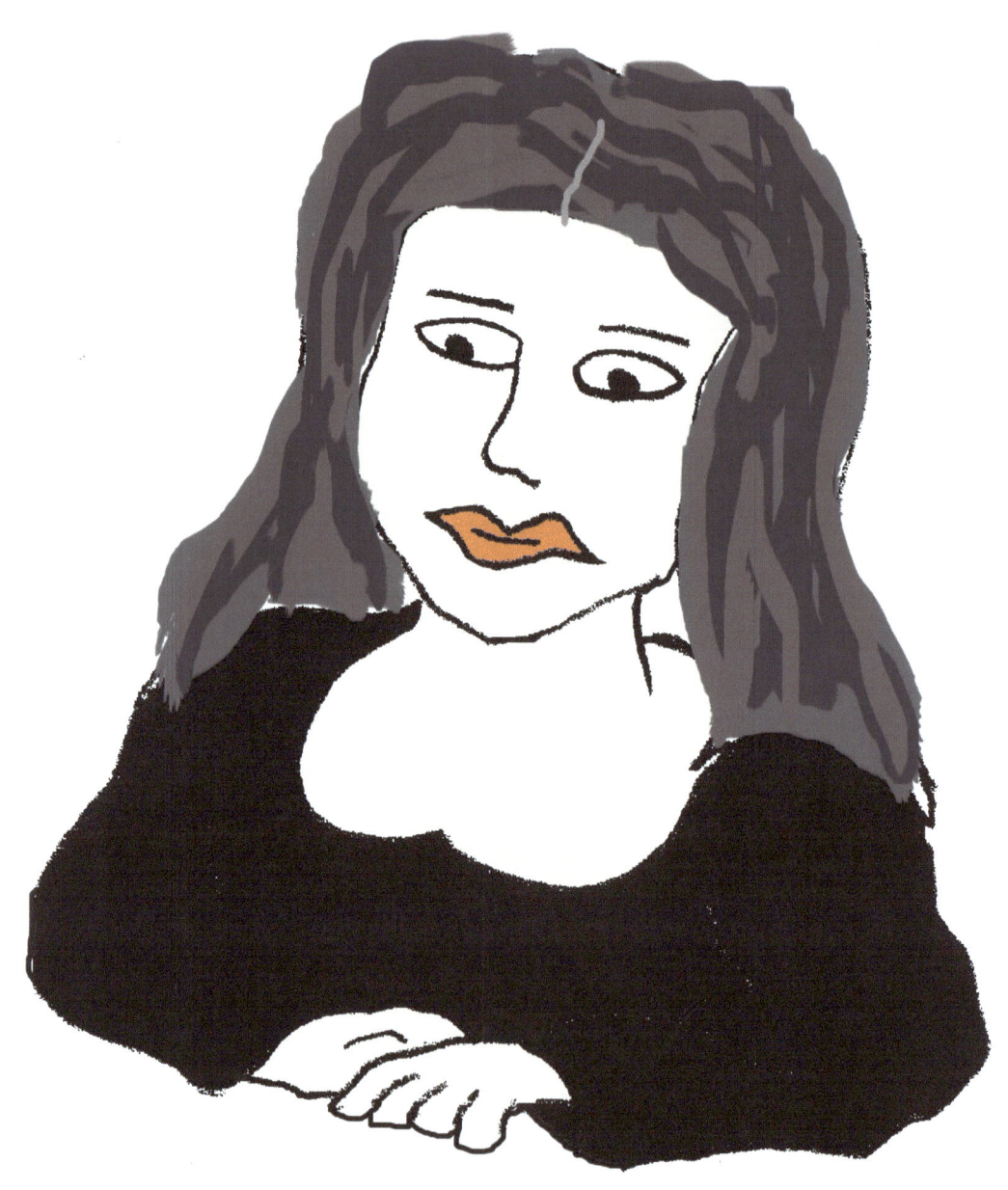

Relaxing for a while with Da Vinci's Mona Lisa,

Winnie couldn't help wondering if Mona liked to eat pizza.

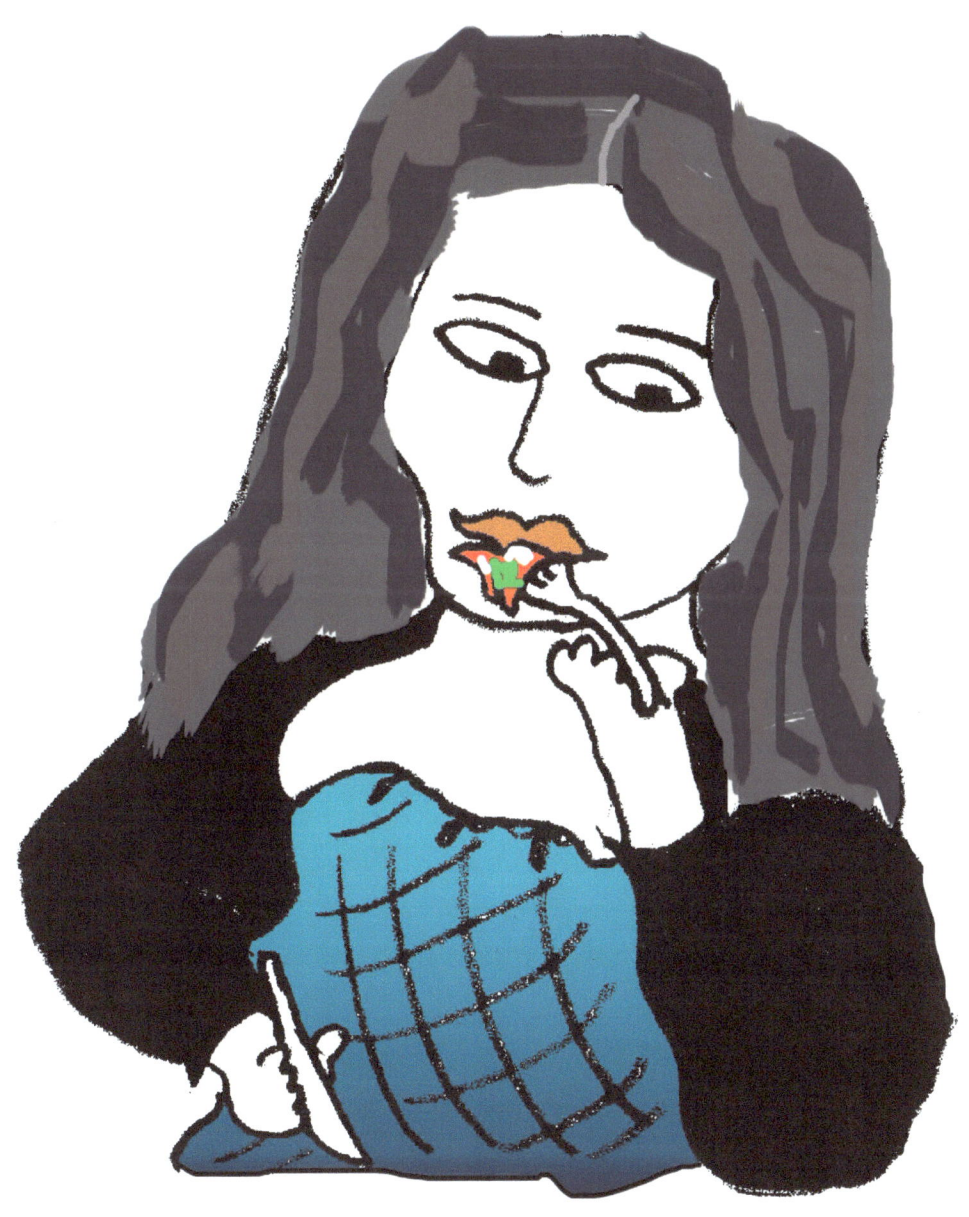

And if she ate pizza would she use a knife and a fork?

Would she have it with onions or olives and pork?

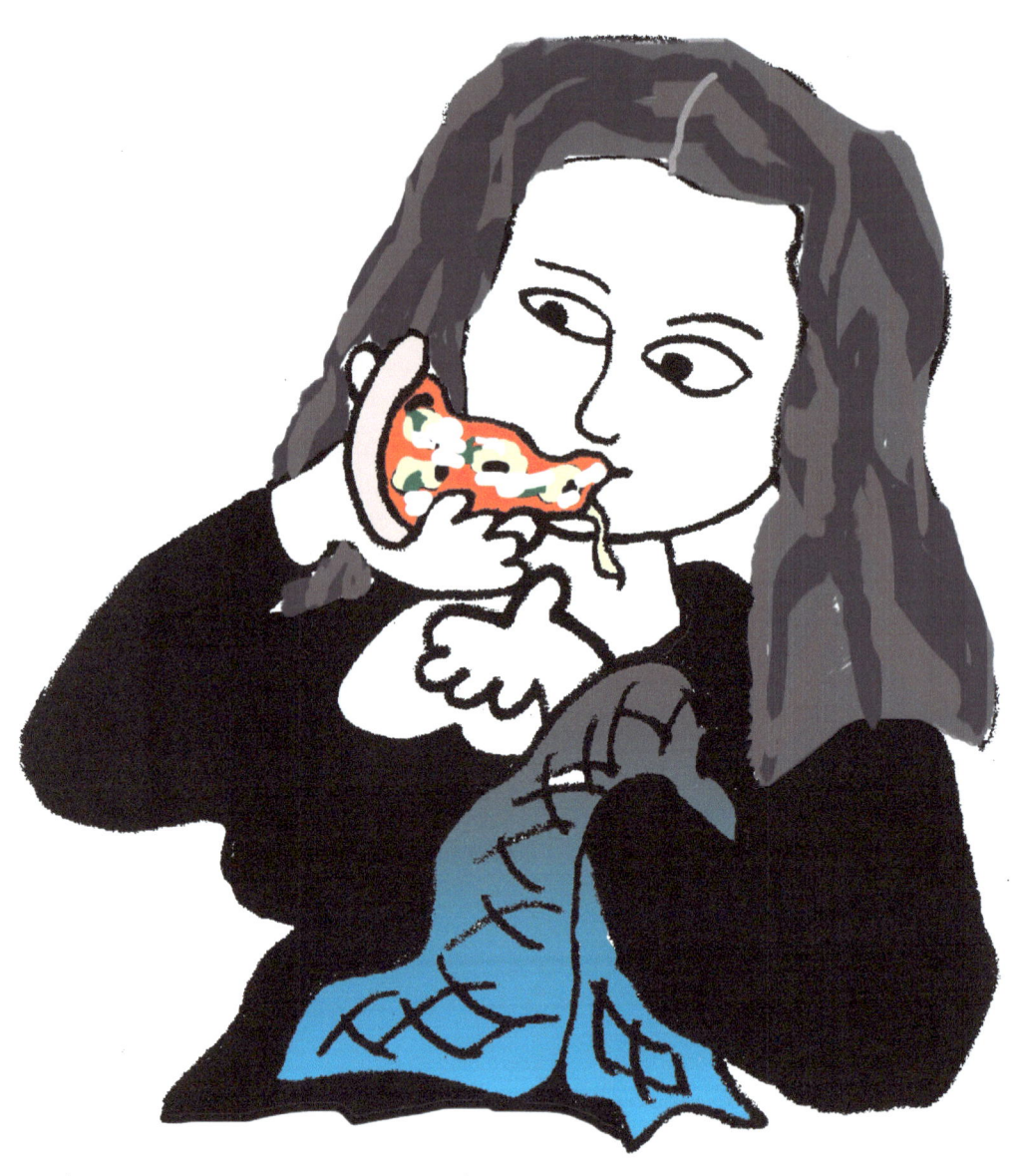

Would Mona have it for breakfast?

Eat it cold or hot?

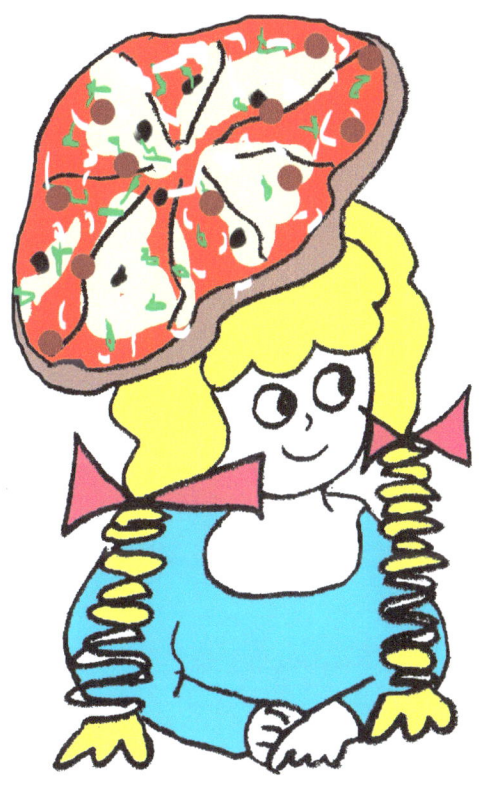

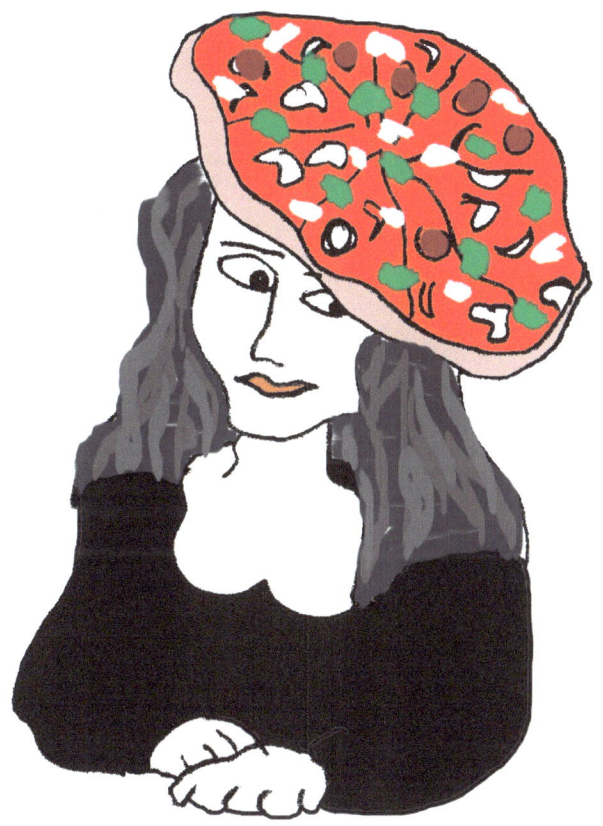

Would she wear it as a hat?

Winnie thought she would not!

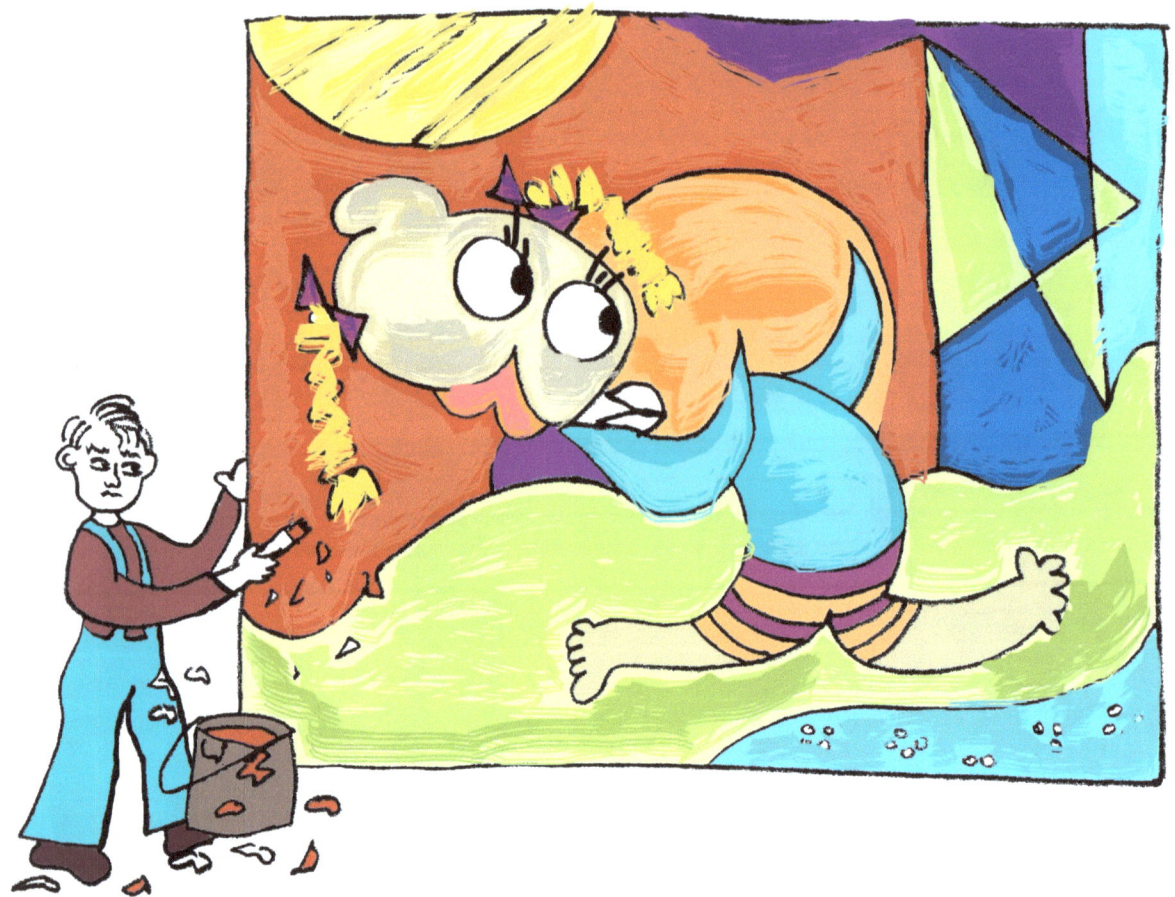

Artist, Pablo Picasso, liked to distort facial features

so that faces of humans looked much more like creatures.

Winnie imagined the way she'd appear,

at the hands of Picasso would she have just one ear?

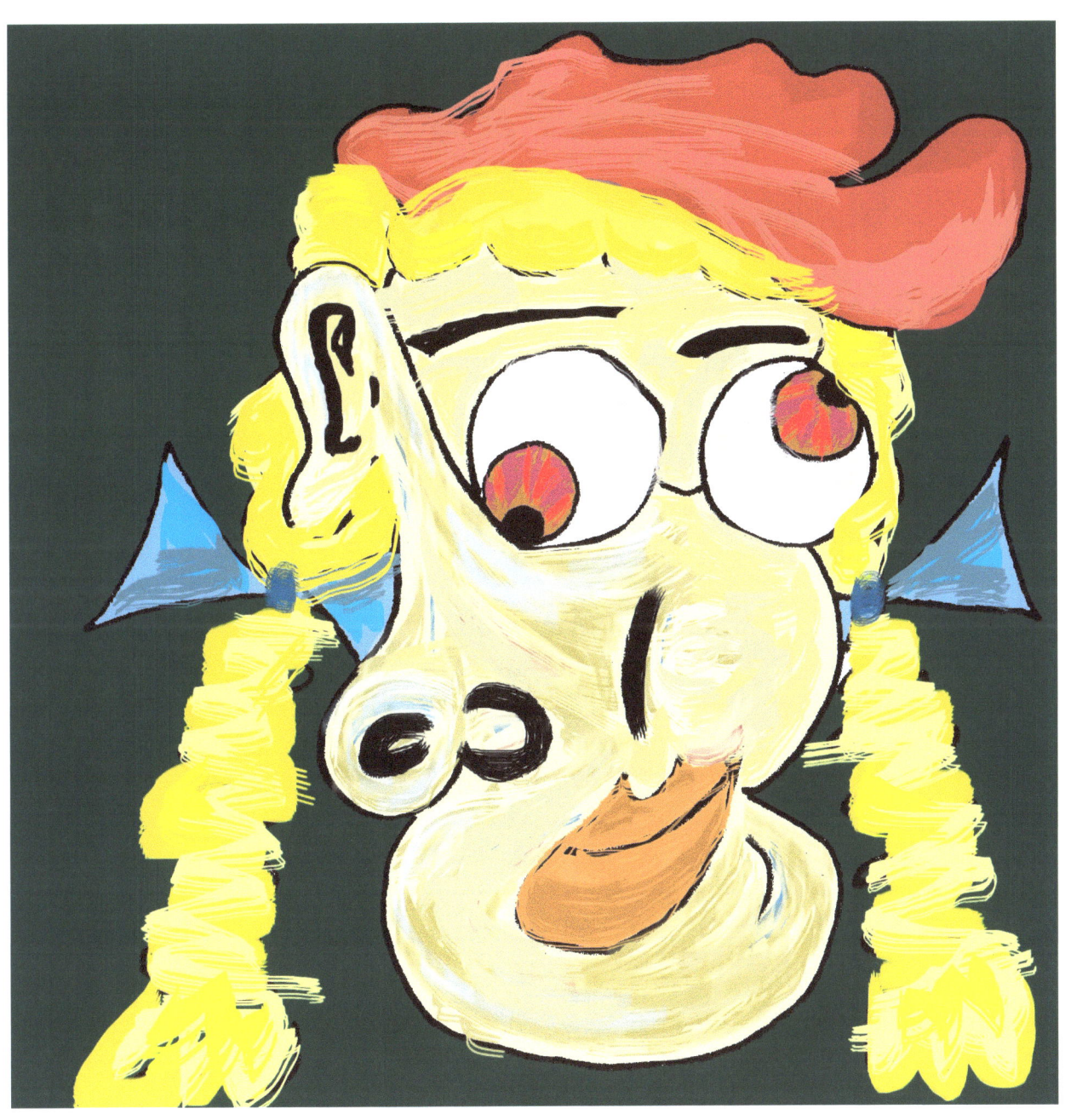

It would be hard to hear, and what if her eyes

were placed sort of crooked and tripled in size?

On second thought, there was a clever disguise.

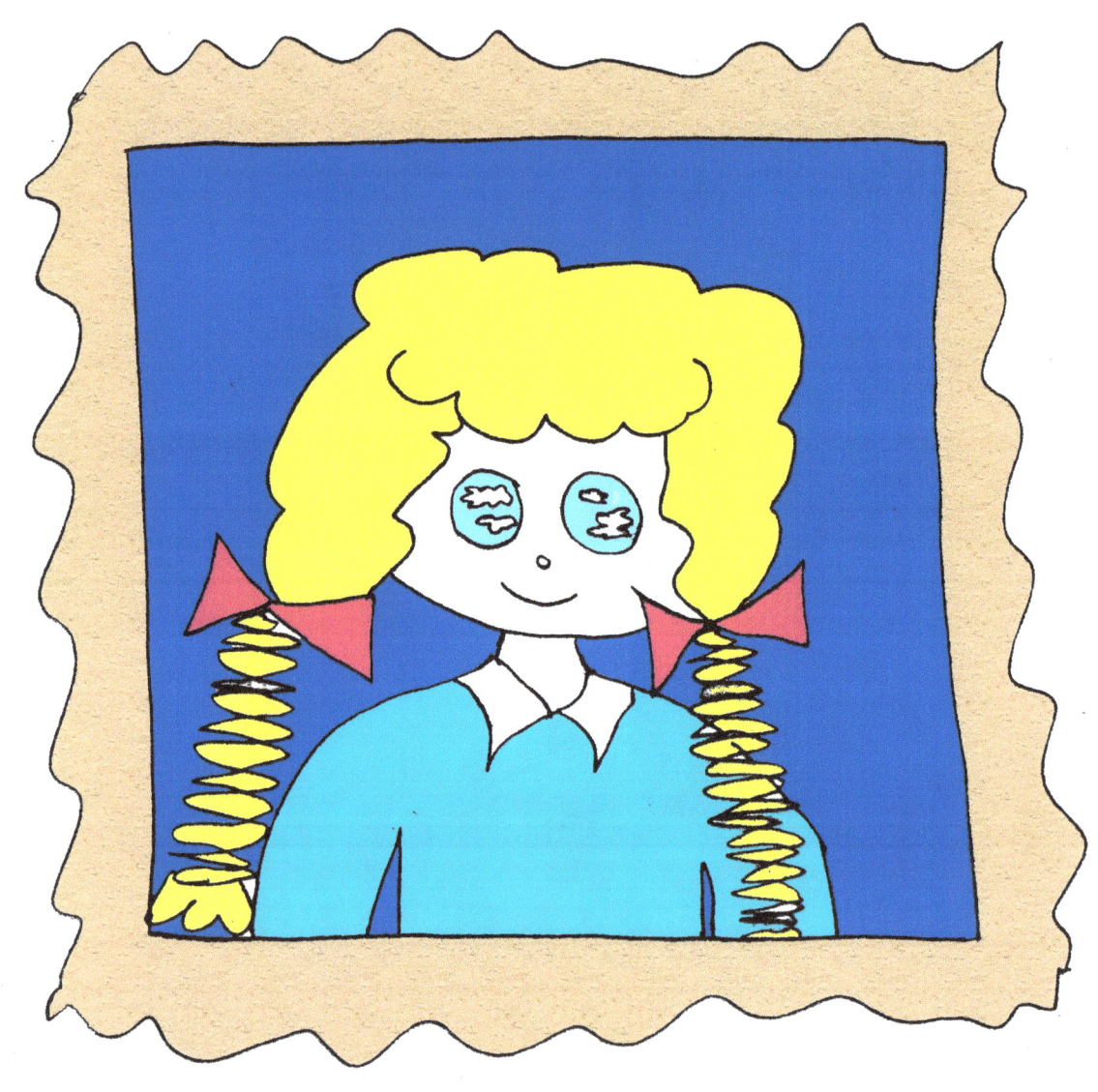

In the surreal world of René Magritte

Winnie's perspective became a little offbeat.

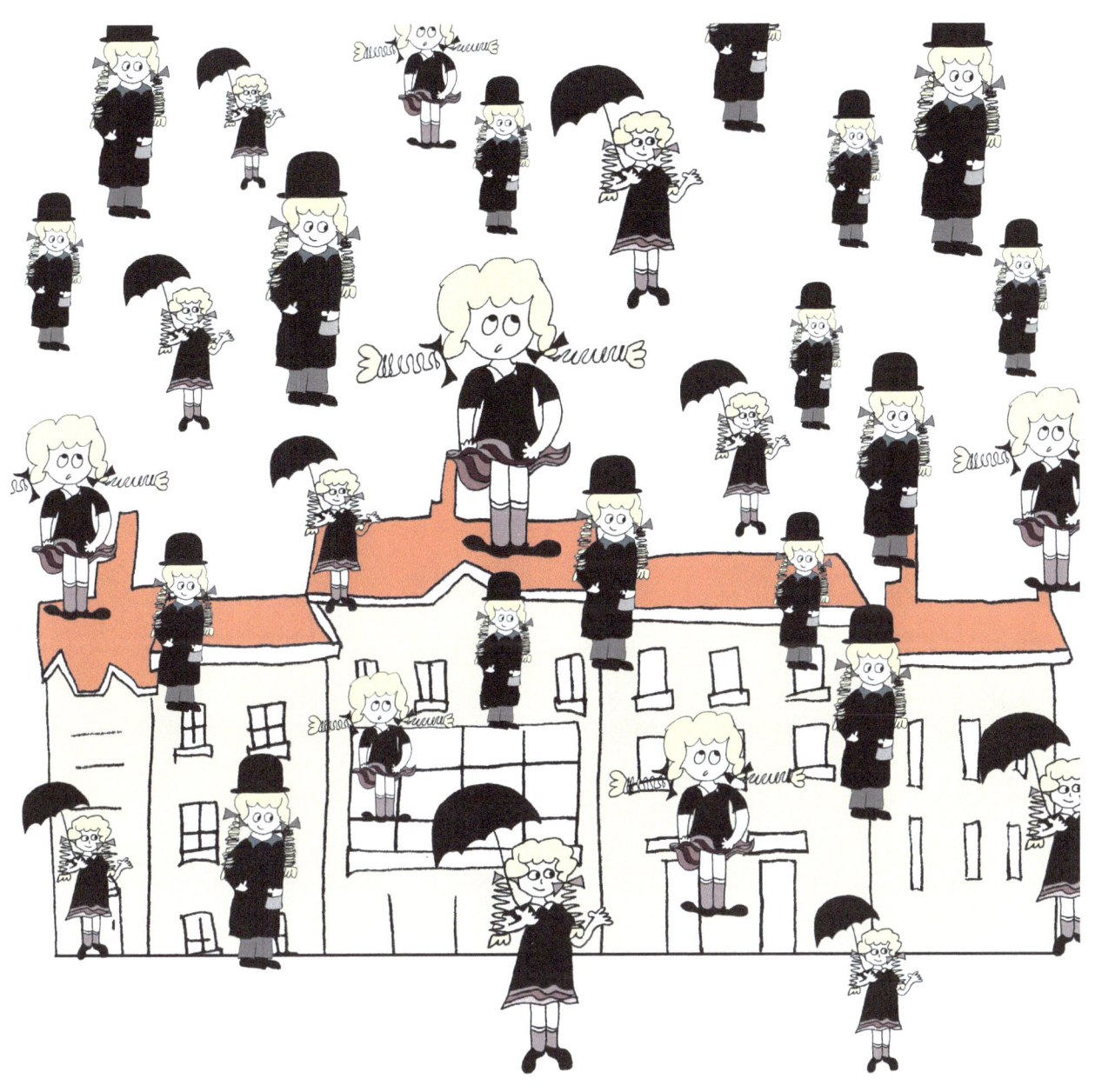

Seeing objects arranged in unusual places

gave her a whole different way of looking at spaces.

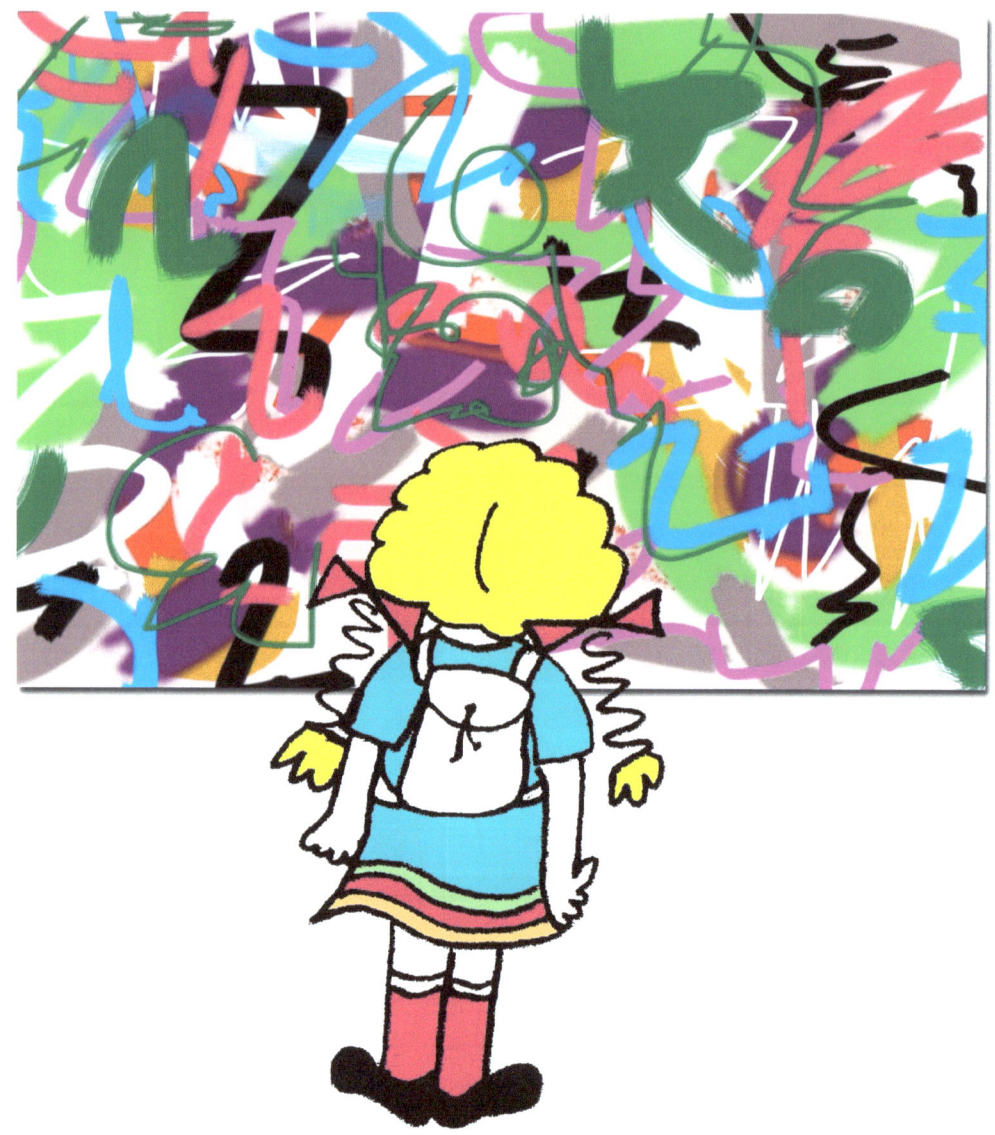

Jackson Pollack, Winnie thought, must have made quite a mess.

How much paint the man used was anyone's guess.

Like fireworks exploding on the fourth of July,

his confetti-like canvas was a treat for the eye.

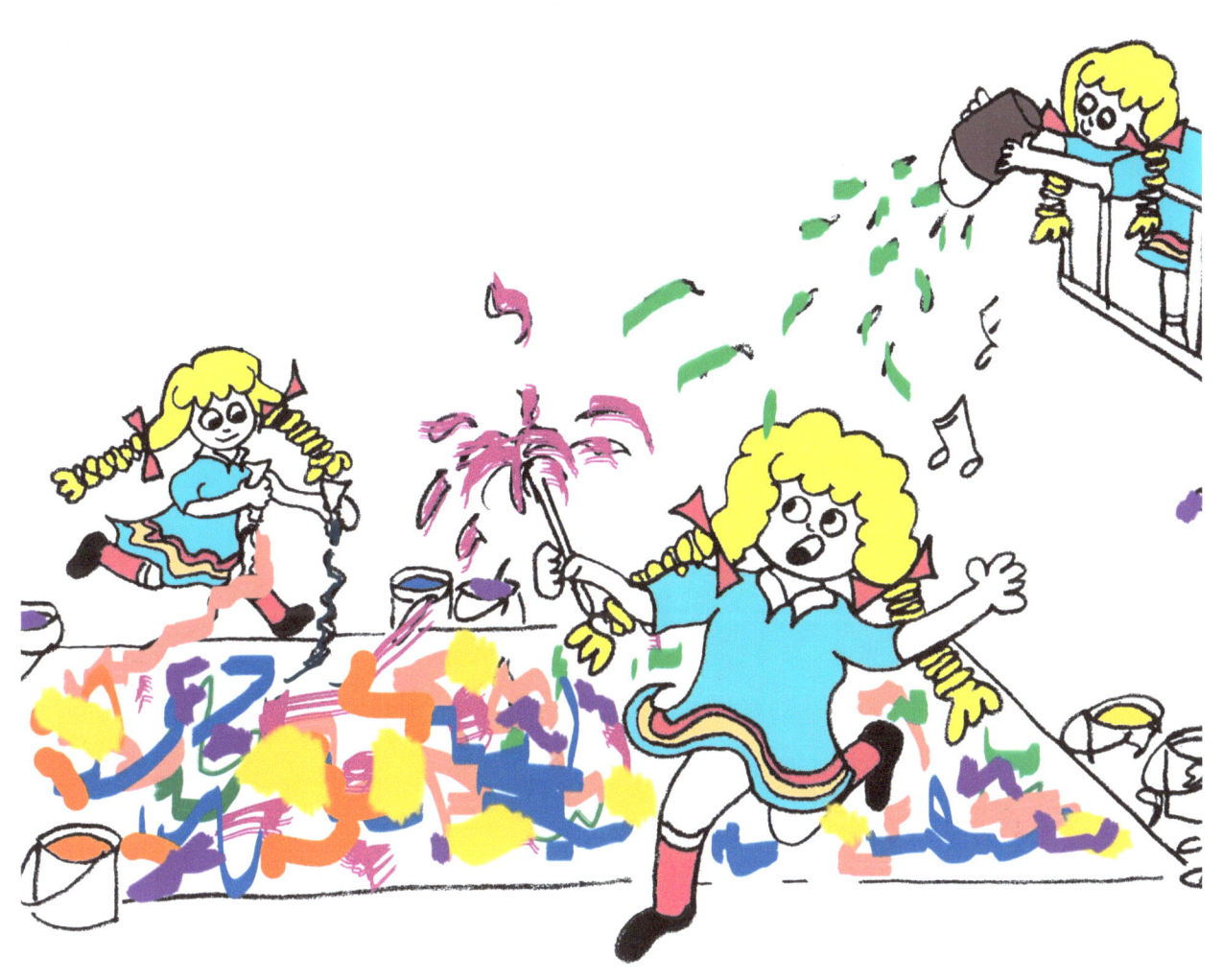

What fun it would be to toss paint everywhere.

Covered in color from your shoes to your hair.

It would be so much fun that you might have to shout,

or sing opera aloud as you hurled paint about.

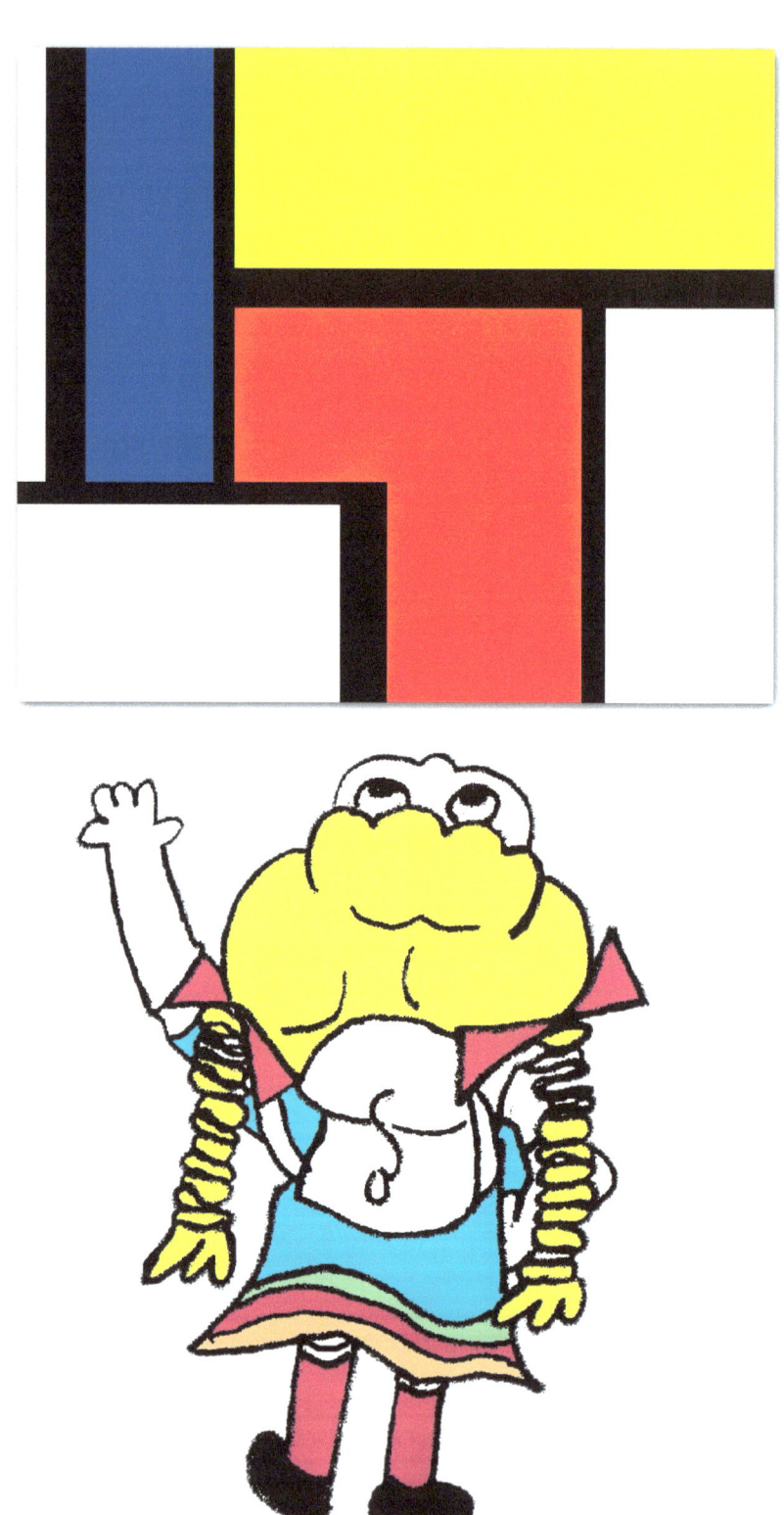

At the Mondrian exhibit, Winnie stared at a square.

She stared and she stared till it looked like a chair.

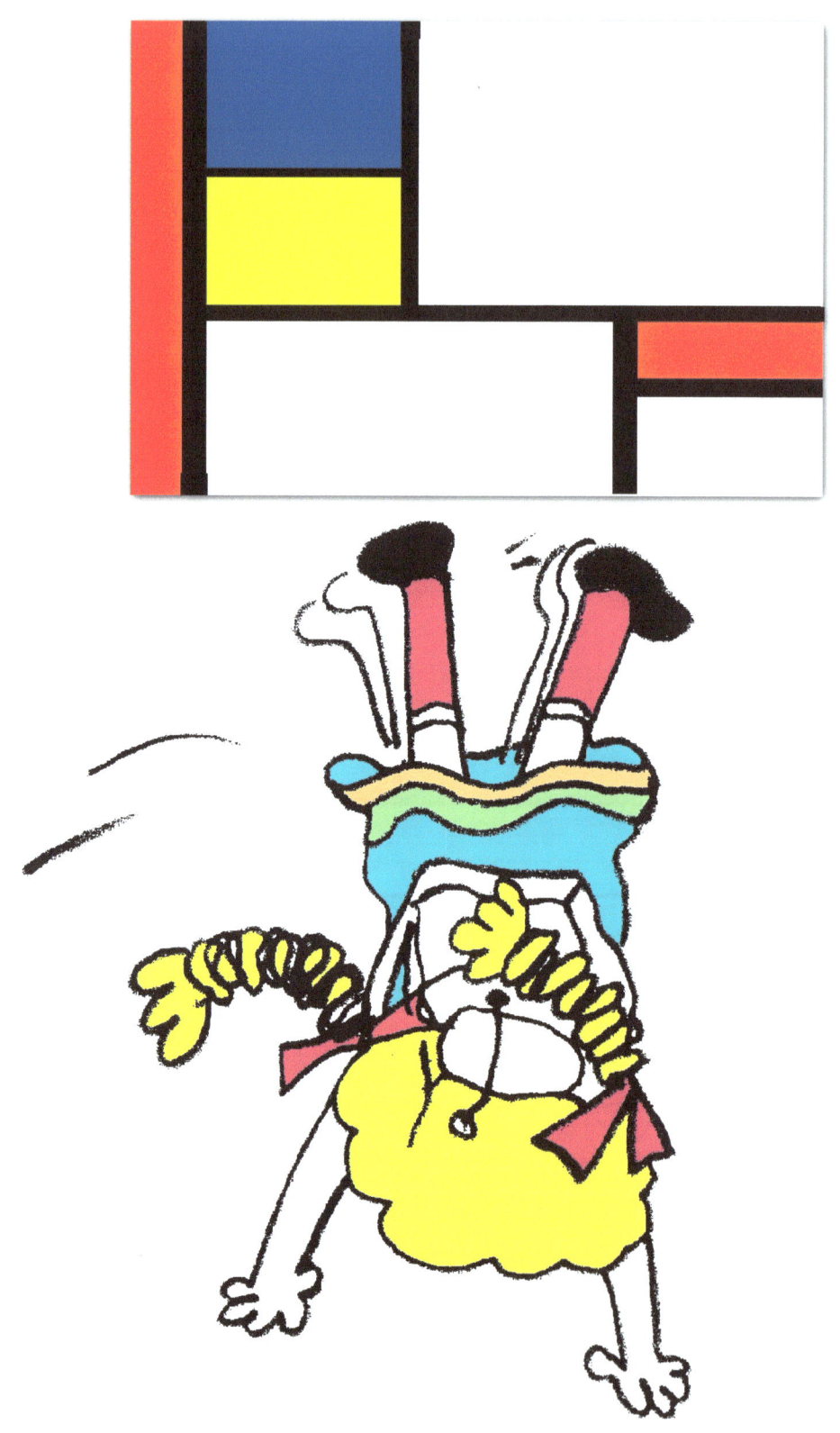

She stared long at lines going every which way.

She stared long at boxes in black, red and gray.

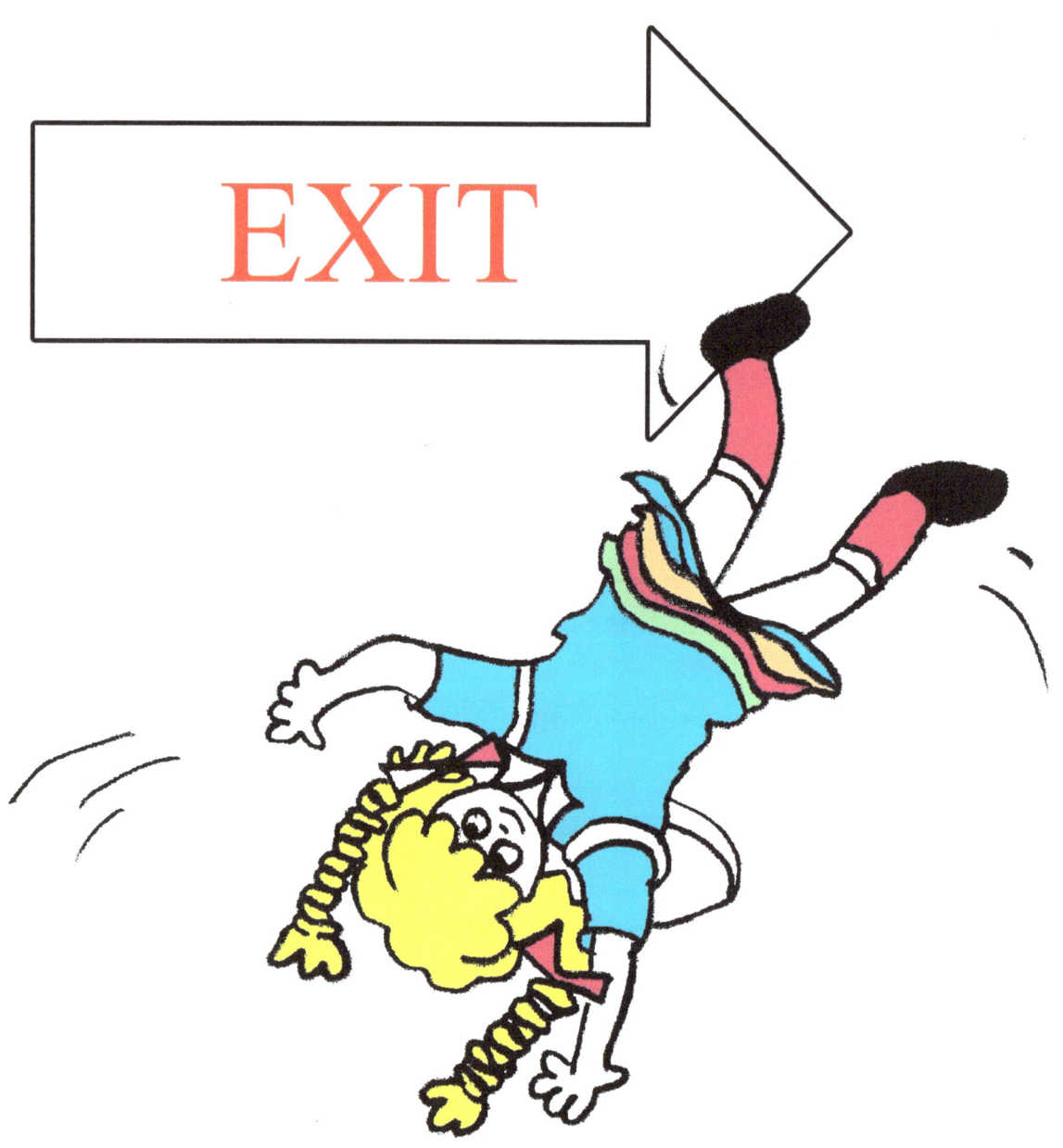

Following lines until one looked familiar,

directing her out of the room that was linear.

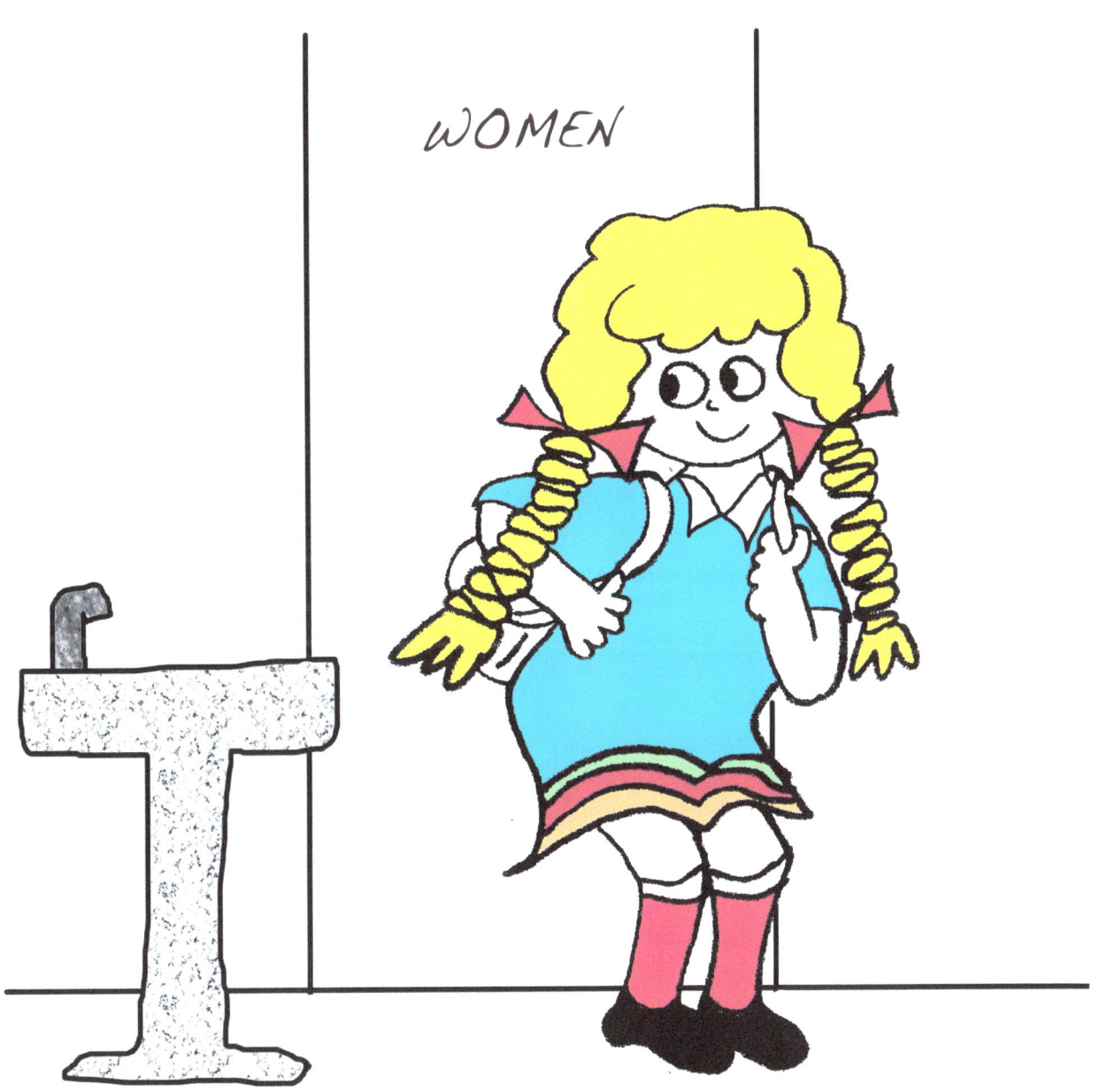

Heading straight for the loo, Winnie soon gave a clue,

confirming for the guard what he already knew.

For the flush of the toilet exposed Winnie to all,

and the guard caught her hiding inside of a stall.

"Now, now," the guard said, "this just isn't right.

You shouldn't be in here, the museum's closed for the night."

"I know," Winnie said, "but I was having such fun

and when the doors closed I just wasn't done."

"Well like you, the art too, must get some rest."

He said, "Come in the day, that really is best."

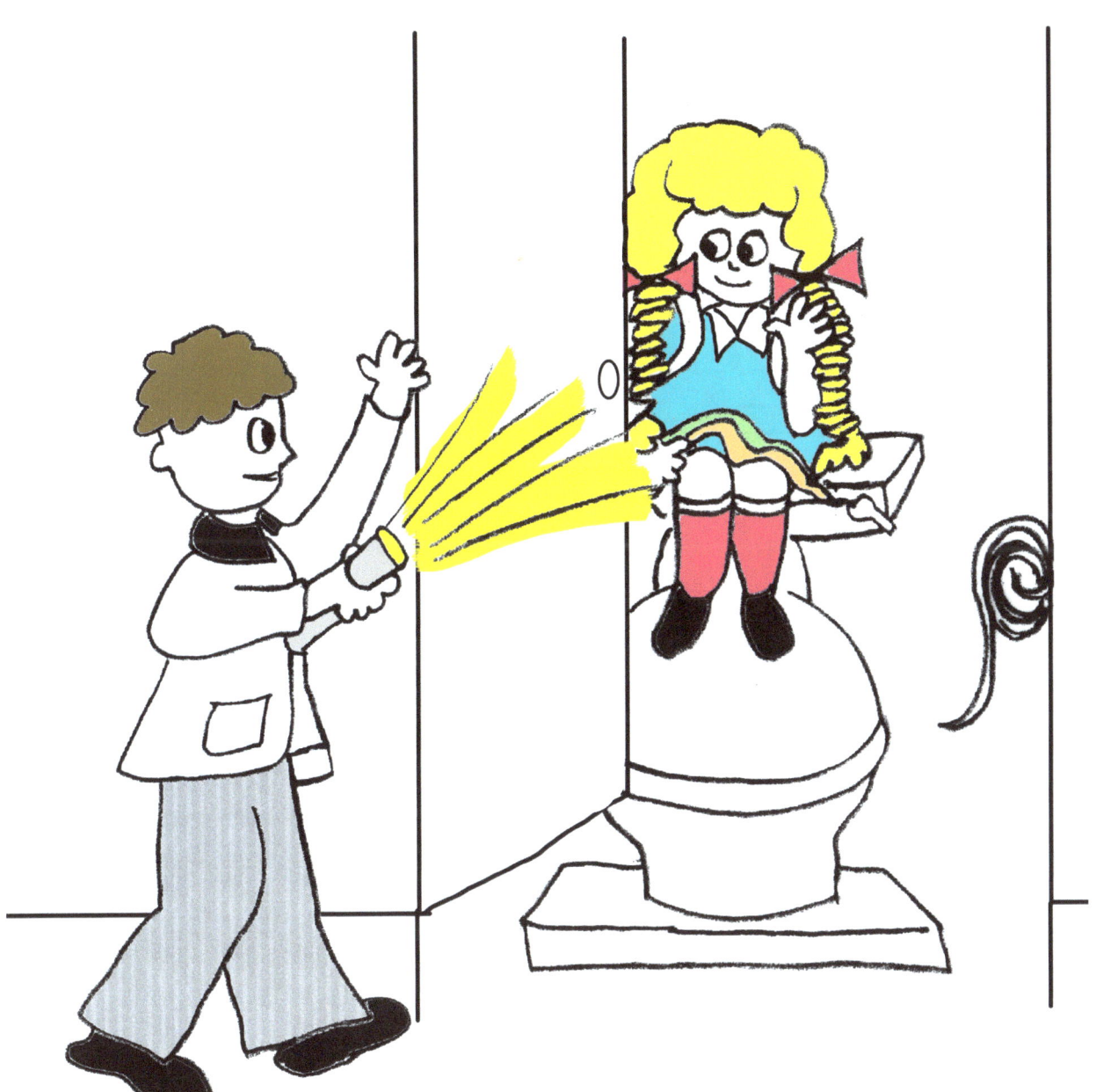

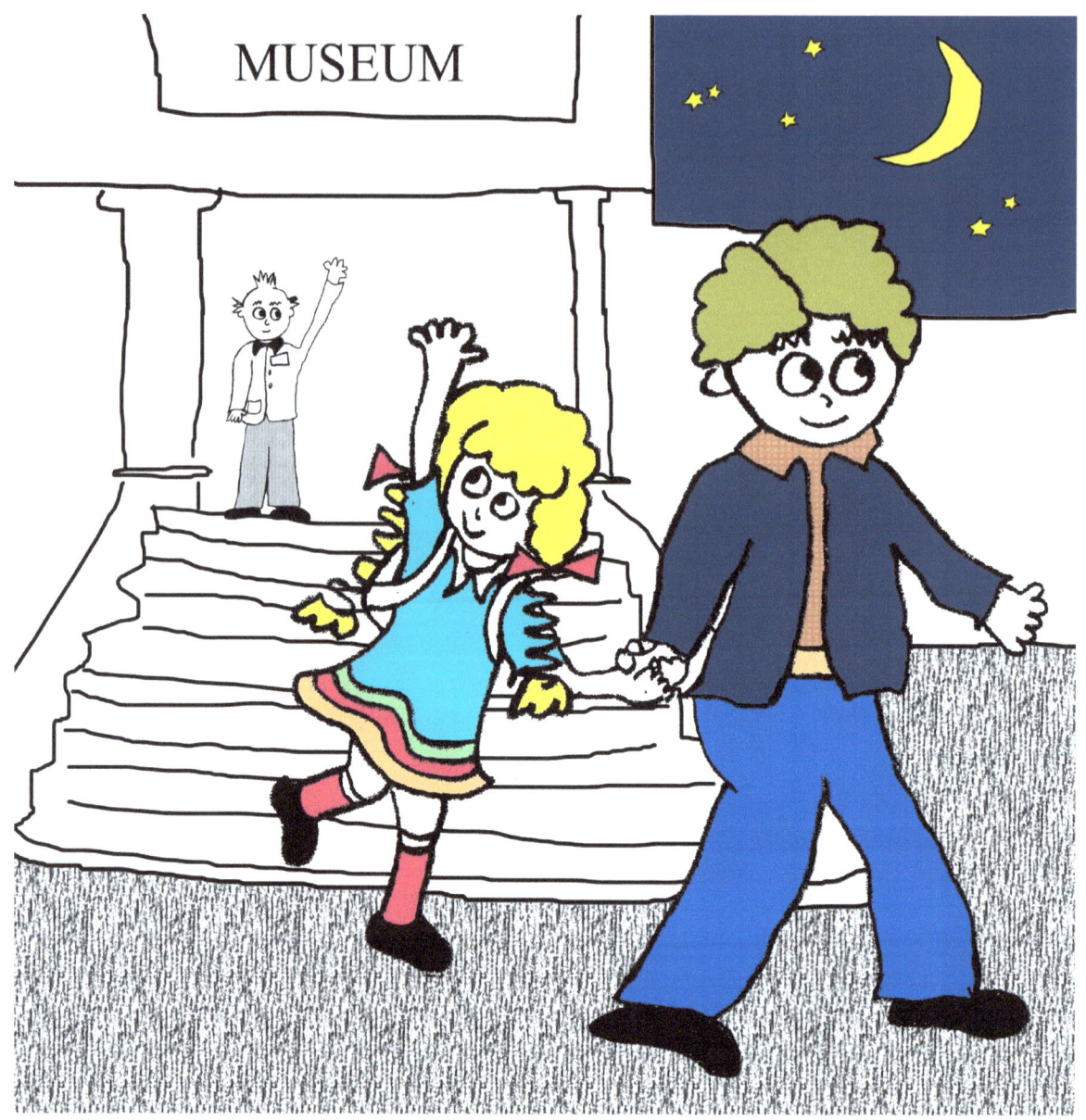

Winnie's dad picked her up from her mini vacation.

Eager to hear Winnie's grand explanation.

And as they headed for home in the light of the moon,

Winnie promised the guard that she'd be back real soon.

THE END

More Books by Leslie Nazarian:

A Happy Halloween

W is for Woofer

Woofer Works Out

Orelda and Corelda on Wall Street

Orelda and Corelda's Ocean Voyage

VISIT US ONLINE AT
LESRUBABOOKS.COM
and
LESRUBADESIGNS.COM

www.ingramcontent.com/pod-product-compliance
Lightning Source LLC
Chambersburg PA
CBHW051103180526
45172CB00002B/752